Ancient Rome

Ancient Rome

VIRGINIA L. CAMPBELL

 Thames & Hudson

Contents

Introduction

The story of Rome can be told as much through its objects as it can be documented in a history book. History provides dates and facts, names and places. However, all of these elements are, fundamentally, about people, both individuals and the mechanisms of a culture as a whole. People produce things: complex works of art that represent the ideology of a ruler, functional tools to kill an enemy or to cook a meal, and personal objects such as a child's doll or a knitted sock. These artefacts, from a lofty marble sculpture to a lowly earthenware bowl, are all part of the history of Roman civilization. This book seeks to present that story, with a detailed examination of some of the artefacts and artwork that are Rome.

Although Rome dominated the Mediterranean for more than one thousand years, it was first established as a small community on the edge of a swamp, struggling against the dominance of another Italic culture, the Etruscans. When Rome was founded by Romulus on the banks of the Tiber River in 753 BCE, the Etruscans were the dominant culture in north and central Italy. Based originally in the north of Italy (present day Tuscany), Etruria was a loose confederation of cities that first came to prominence in the 8th century, becoming rich from mining and trade, and establishing colonies and networks throughout Italy, including with the Greeks of Magna Graecia. As the population of Rome increased and territory began to be added to Roman control, the city was transformed from a backwater to a place of power. This is evidenced in the development of the area now known as the Roman Forum in the 6th century BCE. Within another hundred years, the rule of kings was rejected, thereby expelling the last king, an Etruscan, and founding the Republic, a democratic form of government. This not only drastically changed the governance of Rome, but also marked the beginning of the end for Etruria. Rome made war on its cities, which fell one by one over the next few centuries. The defeat by the Greeks in 474 BCE also ended Etruscan influence in southern Italy (see page 106). Rome was slowly taking control of Italy.

By the 3rd century BCE, Rome had moved beyond Italy and was looking to control the Mediterranean. The Phoenicians of North Africa already dominated sea trade, and conflict was inevitable. Indeed, three Punic Wars were fought over two centuries at sea and by land before Rome was successful in defeating its enemy. The Egadi ram (see page 113) is a remnant of the First Punic War, and the Second left traces of the popularity of Punic general Hannibal, who occupied huge parts of Italy, in the form of his portrait bust (see pages 118–119). By the end of the

Third Punic War, Rome controlled the Mediterranean, and expansion into the territories that bordered the sea followed. The fact that the Romans referred to the Mediterranean Sea as Mare Nostrum (Our Sea) reveals the attitude they held towards their right to rule.

Eventually, Rome was not only a city but also an idea, an empire, a dominant civilization. During the 1st century BCE, the fight to rule Rome led to decades of civil war, assassinations and another change of government, one that relied on the rule of one man. With the rise of Augustus, the Roman empire transformed into the Roman Empire, and the emperor, his wife and his family became the focus (see pages 164–165, 178, 180–181). Succession was established initially through bloodlines, and later by adoption. In both scenarios, there was the potential for power struggles, as seen in 69 CE and 193 CE, when multiple men served as emperor within the space of a single year. Throughout the imperial period, the territory of Rome changed with the addition and loss of provinces as the fortunes of the Empire changed. Britain, for example, was conquered in 43 CE but abandoned in 410 CE as the military was consolidated to more easily defendable locations. The abandonment of provinces is one reason that so many artefacts come from buried hoards (see pages 245–246, 250–253). Issues of succession and rule continued through the 3rd and 4th centuries, despite attempts to share power between two or four men and to split administrative duties between east and west. The increasing popularity of Christianity added further conflict, culminating in the conversion of the first Christian emperor, Constantine (see page 263), and an edict making it the only legal religion of Rome in 395 CE. Within eighty years, the might of Rome was destroyed by invading barbarian tribes and the abandonment of the western half of the Empire.

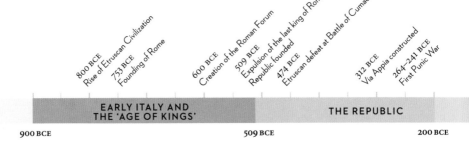

800 BCE
Rise of Etruscan Civilization
753 BCE
Founding of Rome
600 BCE
Creation of the Roman Forum
509 BCE
Expulsion of the last king of Rome;
Republic founded
474 BCE
Etruscan defeat at Battle of Cumae
312 BCE
Via Appia constructed
264–241 BCE
First Punic War

EARLY ITALY AND
THE 'AGE OF KINGS'

THE REPUBLIC

900 BCE   509 BCE   200 BCE

The city of Rome was home to more than one million people in the 2nd century CE, but did not see such numbers again until the late 19th century. While several aspects of Rome continued in the east in the form of the Byzantine empire, what was once the most famous city and most dominant culture in the world was, in effect, lost. However, the buildings and objects made by the Romans remained. In cities such as Rome, Pompeii, Lepcis Magna and Trier, as well as along Hadrian's Wall in Britain, there is clear evidence of Rome and the architecture of an empire. Other remains are located in museums, not only in Italy or former Roman territories, but also the world over. The importance of these artefacts – their study, preservation and accessibility – cannot be overstated. Museums hold objects, and these objects provide the history of Rome.

In this book, approximately 200 artefacts from museum collections around the world are presented in four chronological chapters: Early Italy and the 'Age of Kings', The Republic, Early Empire and Late Empire. The items are arranged thematically within each chapter, and the text explores aspects of society and household, art and personal adornment, politics and warfare, and funerary practices and rituals. Although the works do not adhere to a strict time line within each chapter, the themes allow the exploration of various parts of life in the Roman world, public and private, thereby giving a comprehensive view of the developments of decorative preference, ideology and techniques. As such, these artefacts represent a multi-faceted view of Rome, and provide insight into all aspects of what life was like for the people of Rome, what it meant to be a part of the culture that dominated the Mediterranean and Europe for centuries. The objects are the story of Rome.

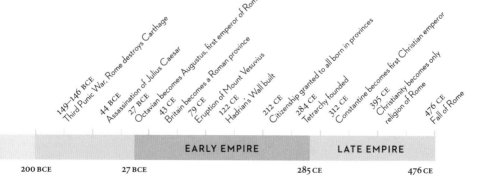

149–146 BCE, Third Punic War, Rome destroys Carthage

44 BCE, Assassination of Julius Caesar

27 BCE, Octavian becomes Augustus, first emperor of Rome

43 CE, Britain becomes a Roman province

79 CE, Eruption of Mount Vesuvius

122 CE, Hadrian's Wall built

212 CE, Citizenship granted to all born in provinces

284 CE, Tetrarchy founded

312 CE, Constantine becomes first Christian emperor

395 CE, Christianity becomes only religion of Rome

476 CE, Fall of Rome

EARLY EMPIRE   LATE EMPIRE

200 BCE   27 BCE   285 CE   476 CE

MAP OF ITALY

Although political domination of Italy
underwent a number of changes in the
centuries between the rise of Etruria and
the fall of Rome, the regions and cities
largely survive, many of them still evident
in place names today.

MAP OF ROMAN EMPIRE
(OVERLEAF)

The greatest geographical extent of the
Roman Empire was reached *c.* 117 CE under
the emperor Trajan, when Rome included
provinces and territory covering most of
Europe, Britain and North Africa, as well
as parts of Asia Minor and the Near East.

Venice

Spina

Bologna

UMBRIA

LIGURIAN
SEA

ETRURIA

Arezzo

PICENUM

Chiusi

Perugia

ADRIATIC
SEA

Vulcii

Viterbo

Cerveteri

Veii

CORSICA

Ostia

Rome

SAMNIUM

LATIUM

Capua

APULIA

CAMPANIA

Naples

Pompeii

Herculaneum

Paestum

Tarentum

LUCIANA

CALABRIA

SARDINIA

TYRRHENIAN
SEA

BRUTIUM

IONIAN
SEA

SICILY

Syracuse

THE ROMAN EMPIRE
c. 117 CE

Vindolanda
Eboracum
BRITANNIA
Londinium
Trier
GAUL
GERMANIA
Lugdunum
HISPANIA
Emerita Augusta
Carthage
MAURETANIA

Rome

ILLYRIUM

DACIA

SARMATIA

BLACK SEA

Constantinople

BITHYNIA
& PONTUS

GREECE

CAPPADOCIA

ARMENIA

Corinth

Athens

Ephesus

Antioch

SYRIA

Palmyra

Syracuse

MEDITERRANEAN
SEA

Lepcis Magna

Cyrene

Jerusalem

Alexandria

Petra

EGYPT

The Beginnings of Rome

A painted, larger-than-life terracotta statue of the god Apollo from the Portonaccio sanctuary of Veii (c. 510–500 BCE, National Etruscan Museum, Villa Giulia, Rome). Apollo and other deities decorated the roof beams of a temple dedicated to the goddess Minerva.

The history of Italy can be simplified as separate groups, cities and people that were eventually unified into a single state. In the ancient period, the earliest well-documented dominant political and cultural group was the Etruscans.

The Etruscans lived in north-central Italy, in land between the Tiber and Arno Rivers. Excellent seafarers, they flourished in the 8th through 6th centuries BCE, when much profit was made from trade and colonization. They lived in fortified cities built on hill-tops, such as Tarquinia, Cerveteri, Vulci and Veii. Their influence can be found throughout the Italian peninsula. Yet, it is difficult to conceive of Etruria as a single state – more an interconnected collection of cities with shared language, religion and art.

At the outset, Etruscan art was heavily influenced by Greek art but, as it developed, it had a reciprocal impact on Greek art in southern Italy, as well as on the art and architecture of Rome. Mining tin, copper, iron and silver in the hills of Italy turned the Etruscans into accomplished metalworkers. Many of the statues and decorative

Bronze statue of the Capitoline She-Wolf with Romulus and Remus (c. 450–430 BCE, Capitoline Museums, Rome), illustrating part of the foundation myth of Rome that the abandoned twins were suckled by a wolf.

architectural elements were made of terracotta, which was typically painted. Although many luxury art, jewelry and other objects were imported from Greece, Egypt and points further east, there was localized production that combined a mix of Orientalizing and native Italic motifs.

The fall of Etruria can be charted in a series of events from the late 6th century BCE onwards. Etruscan cities fell to Rome one by one over the course of a century. In part, their lack of a centralized political unit was their undoing, as they could not mount a successfully unified defence against the rising power of Rome.

Rome's origin and rise are steeped in mythology, which tells the story of twin boys raised by a she-wolf, one of whom, the titular Romulus, would go on to found the city on seven hills. Initially, the Eternal City was simply a collection of Iron Age huts on the Palatine Hill. Slowly, the city grew, incorporating nearby tribes, waging war against other Latins and, if the stories are to be believed, using a fair bit of trickery as well. From the founding of the city, Rome was

Etruscan tumulus tombs from the Banditaccia Necropolis in Cerveteri. Subterranean multi-chambered tombs were cut into tufa, a soft volcanic rock, and then covered with earthen mounds.

ruled by kings. Beginning with Romulus, there were seven in total. The fifth king, Lucius Tarquinius Priscus, ruling from 616 BCE to 578 BCE, was the first Etruscan king, beginning an hereditary line that would end with the expulsion of his grandson Lucius Tarquinius Superbus and all kings in 509 BCE. It was then that Rome became a republic, changing forever the culture, government, art, military and idea of what it meant to be a Roman.

Roman art is somewhat difficult to define – it borrows, copies and adopts from many Mediterranean cultures – making something that is sometimes indistinguishable from the original and sometimes entirely new and unique. Influences can be seen from Greek and Egyptian art, as well as Etruscan, Near Eastern, North African and native Italic forms. The earliest years of Roman art are difficult to distinguish from Etruscan art, and likely much of it was produced in the same studios or by artists trained in the same technique. It is in the years following the creation of the Republic in 509 BCE that Roman art becomes a distinct and recognizable form.

Etruscan bobbin

c. 600–500 BCE

*Bucchero • Length: 4 cm (1½ in.), Diameter: 1.1 cm (½ in.)
• From Chiusi, Tuscany, Italy*

BRITISH MUSEUM, LONDON, UK

This burnished pottery bobbin, used for winding wool
or thread, is indicative of the importance of wool work
and textile production in Etruria. Small items, such as
this bobbin, were often included in burial and were,
for the most part, gender specific. Women were buried
with spinning and weaving tools, whereas male graves
had deposits of weaponry or agricultural tools. In some
instances, where small female items, like spindle whorls
or fibulae, are discovered in a grave that otherwise
appears male, it could be a token offering made by
a female family member at the time of burial.

Etruscan lebes gamikos

c. 725–700 BCE
Terracotta • Height: 57 cm (22½ in.),
width: 43 cm (17 in.) • From Vulci,
Montalto di Castro, Lazio, Italy

ART INSTITUTE OF CHICAGO, USA

The lebes, a Greek form, is a deep bowl
with no handles, and one of the oldest shapes
produced in black figure pottery. This version, a lebes gamikos,
differs in that it has handles, a lid and is made with an elongated
neck and stand. It was typically used in marriage ceremonies,
and Greek versions often depict scenes of the bride or wedding.
This vessel was made locally in Etruria, adapting the Greek
form and painting it with neutral geometric patterns in
a manner more in line with the native aesthetic.

Etruscan flask

c. 725–700 BCE
*Bronze • Height: 16 cm (6¼ in.), diameter: 11 cm
(4¼ in.) • From Vulci, Montalto di Castro, Lazio, Italy*
NATIONAL ETRUSCAN MUSEUM, VILLA GIULIA,
ROME, ITALY

Remarkably similar in shape and design to a modern
canteen for carrying water, this bronze pilgrim flask
is reinforced on the seams, has a chain attaching the
cap to the body of the container and a hinged handle
for carrying. Although a purely functional item,
some attempt to decorate the flask has been made
by creating concentric circles of raised dots on the
body of the container. The skill with which the small
elements of the chain, attachments and seams have
been manufactured demonstrates the fine metalwork
techniques practised in Vulci, even for basic items
such as this.

Statuette of a young woman

late 6th century BCE

Bronze • Height: 29.5 cm (11½ in.) • From Vulci, Montalto di Castro, Lazio, Italy

METROPOLITAN MUSEUM OF ART, NEW YORK CITY, USA

This statuette shows a clear influence from the Greek tradition of korai: free-standing statues of young women (or men: koroui). Elements copied from the Greek type include the frontal pose with the right hand extended, the left holding the edge of the clothing and what is known as the 'Archaic smile'. The details of the hair, necklace, patterns in the fabric and shoes on the statue's front seem to have taken precedence over accurate detail in the round – there are no folds or detail in the dress on the figure's rear. The pointed shoes with laces and floral ornament are distinctively Etruscan.

Vase in the shape of a cockerel

c. 630–620 BCE
Bucchero • Height: 10.3 cm (4 in.) • From Viterbo, Lazio, Italy
METROPOLITAN MUSEUM OF ART,
NEW YORK CITY, USA

This small pot, shaped like a cockerel, is made of bucchero (a fine black clay that, when fired, resembles bronze), with details of the bird's feathers, wings and crown incised. It is surmised it was used to hold ink, with the head used as a stopper that could be attached to the body with a cord. What is remarkable about this vase, however, is that the twenty-six letters of the Etruscan alphabet are inscribed on the base. Etruscan is neither an Indo-European language, as other Italic languages, nor is it Semitic, like Phoenician or Aramaic. The Etruscans adapted the earliest Greek alphabet brought to Italy in the 8th century BCE, and typically wrote in retrograde, from right to left, however this example displays text written from left to right.

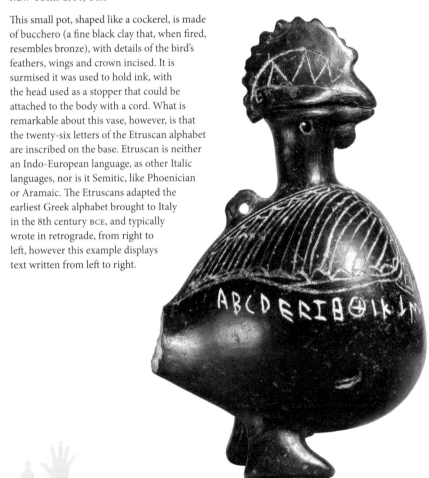

Kantharos

mid 7th century BCE

Impasto • Height: 7.5 cm (3 in.), width: 12.7 cm (5 in.) • From a tomb at Narce, near Civita Castellana, Lazio, Italy

UNIVERSITY OF PENNSYLVANIA MUSEUM OF ARCHAEOLOGY AND ANTHROPOLOGY, PHILADELPHIA, USA

The two-handled, deep-bowled, drinking vessel with a trumpet-shaped foot known as a kantharos is, despite the Greek name, an indigenous Italic shape. It was so popular for drinking wine that it is often used by Dionysus, god of wine, in artistic representations. Examples have been found in bronze as well as impasto, and it retains certain features of metal production. This example has six countersunk discs cut into the clay for bronze studs, which were either never added or are now lost.

Chalice

c. 590–560 BCE

Bucchero • Height: 15.1 cm (6 in.),
diameter (rim): 16.8 cm (6½ in.),
diameter (base): 11 cm (4¼ in.)
• From Tarquinia, Viterbo, Lazio, Italy

BRITISH MUSEUM,
LONDON, UK

The chalice is related to the indigenous Etruscan form of the kantharos (see opposite), the major difference being the lack of handles. Bucchero items made of shiny black pottery, seen as imitations of Etruscan metalwork, were originally rare and highly prized items, found only in the princely tombs of the 7th century, but by the 6th century BCE they had become standardized in form and were being exported across the Mediterranean. This chalice is decorated with a roller-stamped frieze depicting a winged figure and a duck, animals and a sphinx.

Antefix of a female figure

c. 520–510 BCE

Terracotta • Height: 17.1 cm (6¾ in.),
length: 30.2 cm (12 in.) • From Caere, Lazio, Italy

METROPOLITAN MUSEUM OF ART,
NEW YORK CITY, USA

An antefix (roof tile) such as this would have been
placed at the corner of a building to act as a conduit for
rainwater, channelling run-off into an opening behind
the head. Painted as a female figure wearing a diadem,
the woman has black wavy hair, large disc earrings and
a necklace of small pendants. The diadem is decorated
with white palmettes and volutes against a dark red
background. It is unclear if the antefix represents
a mythological figure or a mortal woman, but the
decoration and jewels depicted indicate a woman
of wealth. Unlike Greek and, to
an extent, later Roman women,
Etruscan women enjoyed a
high level of independence,
including the ability to own
property and businesses
without the oversight
of a male guardian.

Etruscan pendant with swastika symbols

c. 700–650 BCE
Gold • Diameter: 8 cm (3 in.)
• From Bolsena, near Montefiascone, Lazio, Italy

LOUVRE, PARIS, FRANCE

A large gold pendant decorated in repoussé; it is banded with geometric designs, punctuated with birds, and the centre of the disc features five concentric circles interspersed with swastikas. The swastika is an ancient symbol, used by multiple cultures for thousands of years as a symbol for health and good luck. It features regularly in repetitive patterns on pottery and mosaics. A fold of metal at the top of the pendant creates a tube by which the pendant would have been strung on a chain to wear.

Bracelet

c. 650–600 BCE

Gold • Dimensions: unknown • From Regolini-Galassi Tomb, Caere, Lazio, Italy

GREGORIAN ETRUSCAN MUSEUM, VATICAN MUSEUMS, ROME, ITALY

Originally one of a pair, this wide, cuff-like gold bracelet was one of the many gold items found in the rich Regolini-Galassi Tomb (see page 56). The bracelet is decorated in a repeating pattern depicting a female figure between two lions and palm trees, with geometric bands creating a border on the outer edges of the cuff. Two techniques of metalwork, granulation (the application of small beads of gold soldered together) and repoussé, were used to produce this piece, demonstrating the high quality of metalwork for which Etruscan workshops were known.

TRIDACNA SQUAMOSA SHELL COSMETIC VESSEL

c. 630–580 BCE

Shell • Height: 13.7 cm (5¼ in.), width: 21.7 cm (8½ in.), depth: 11 cm (4¼ in.) • From Vulci, Montalto di Castro, Lazio, Italy

BRITISH MUSEUM, LONDON, UK

Tridacna shells originate in the Red Sea and they have been found in excavations in the Near East and Greece. The shells were used both as they appeared naturally and worked into a design, such as this example. Most of the shells carved into a design have been found in religious contexts, as offerings left in sanctuaries dedicated to female deities. It is believed that the tradition of carving the shells comes from the Palestinian/Syrian region of the Levant.

This shell, found in Vulci, has a human head at the apex and the interior is decorated with sphinxes, lotus flowers and triangles. It was probably used as a receptacle for cosmetics. Real shells and shell motifs were not uncommon features of containers for cosmetics, perfume or other beauty items. This is likely due to the association of Aphrodite (also known as Venus), the goddess of love and beauty, with the sea and shells.

Although the exact context of this find is unknown, it was probably a burial deposit in the tomb of a woman. This shell is the only one of its kind found in the Western Mediterranean, which indicates the incredible wealth of whoever had it in her possession.

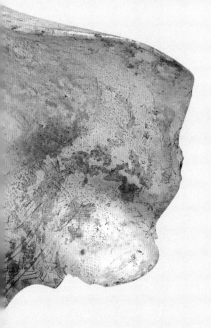

Silver shell cosmetic holder with a goddess riding a sea-monster in relief on the lid. From the colonies of Magna Graecia in southern Italy (c. 3rd century BCE).

Straight pin

late 6th century BCE

Gold and glass • Length: 6.4 cm (2½ in.) • From Italy

CLEVELAND MUSEUM OF ART, USA

This simple, straight pin with a red glass bead embellishing the top would have been used to fasten clothing. Pins such as this could be used by either men or women. The bead is held in place with small triangular prongs and the bezel decorated with a rope. The stem of the pin is twisted, which may have been done purposefully in order to better hold a garment in place. Coloured glass beads or paste, often imitating gemstones or other semi-precious stones, were a common feature of Etruscan jewelry.

Perfume bottle

early 6th century BCE
*Terracotta • Height: 11 cm (4¼ in.),
width: 6.4 cm (2½ in.) • From Vulci,
Montalto di Castro, Lazio, Italy*

BRITISH MUSEUM, LONDON, UK

Although found in Vulci, this perfume
bottle was manufactured in Greece, and
is another example of the importation
of goods to Etruria. Shaped and
decorated in the form of a man in
an Orientalizing style, the bottle is
painted to provide further detail.
Colour is used for hair, necklace, eyes,
mouth and nipples. White dots on the
forehead indicate a diadem or band
around the head, similar to the detail
on the necklace. Anthropomorphic
jars and containers were fairly
common, but the detail on this
one – such as the shape of the chest
and ribcage – is exceptional.

Silver gilt ring

c. 550 BCE

Gold and silver • Length of bezel: 1.6 cm (¾ in.)
• From Vulci, Montalto di Castro, Lazio, Italy

METROPOLITAN MUSEUM OF ART,
NEW YORK CITY, USA

The bezel of this ring is a cartouche, depicting
three animals created by intaglio. The top and central
register both contain hybrid creatures of Greek mythology:
a chimera (a fire-breathing hybrid animal usually depicted
as a winged lion with the head of a goat rising from its back
and a snake's head on the tail) and a siren (famed singers with
the body of a bird and head of a woman). The lower register
depicts a flying scarab beetle. The chosen figures are a mix of
Greek, Egyptian and Phoenician motifs. This is indicative
of the multicultural influence on Etruscan art.

Ring with sphinx
and two birds

c. 550–500 BCE

Gold • Length of cartouche: 2 cm (¾ in.)
• From Ferentinum, near Viterbo, Lazio, Italy

MUSEUM OF FINE ARTS, BOSTON, USA

Found in a tomb with a collection of
items, this gold ring has a bezel made in
the shape of a cartouche. The cartouche
is divided into three registers. The
two outer registers contain birds
with spread wings, while the central
register features a sphinx holding a
branch and wearing a hat. This hat
resembles those worn by haruspices,
men who were trained in the art of
divination and who read the entrails
of sacrificed animals, such as sheep,
for omens. This was a practice of
Etruscan religion that was adopted
and continued by the Romans.

Etruscan disc earrings

late 6th century BCE

Gold • Diameter: 4.8 cm (1¾ in.) • From Caere, Lazio, Italy

J. PAUL GETTY MUSEUM, LOS ANGELES, USA

These large disc earrings are an excellent example of the fine metalwork of Etruscan jewelry. On a backing piece of gold sheet are six rosettes surrounding a central disc with a raised point. The outer edge of each earring is further decorated with six human heads. The heads are made by repoussé, the rosettes by granulation and there is further embellishment with filigree. A hollow gold tube projects from the back to fit into pierced ears, which would have been held in place using a pin in a loop at the end of the tube. Earrings such as this are not only found as objects, but feature as adornment on women in paintings and on vases of the same period.

Faliscan cuirass

c. 725–700 BCE

Bronze • Height: 47 cm (18½ in.), width: 45 cm (17¾ in.) • From the Tomb of the Warrior, Narce, near Civita Castellana, Lazio, Italy

UNIVERSITY OF
PENNSYLVANIA MUSEUM
OF ARCHAEOLOGY
AND ANTHROPOLOGY,
PHILADELPHIA, USA

This cuirass (breastplate) is made of a single sheet of bronze, rolled at the edges and decorated using the technique of repoussé (pressing or hammering into shape). Only the front half remains, although a small tab for fastening it to the rear plate remains on the left side. The front of the plate is contoured into a central peak, with decoration of wolf's teeth and bosses (raised circles) in bands. Found in a tomb named for the large deposit of armaments, it is in the typical style of late Villanovan metalwork. The design of the plate and the decoration is unusual, with no close parallels, suggesting the owner was not an average soldier, but of high rank.

Sword and scabbard

c. 8th century BCE

Bronze • Length of sword: 40 cm (15¾ in.)
• From Necropolis of Mandrione di Cavalupo,
Vulci, Montalto di Castro, Lazio, Italy

NATIONAL ETRUSCAN MUSEUM,
VILLA GIULIA, ROME, ITALY

Etruscan swords were typically short,
stabbing weapons with a straight iron blade,
often with a wooden or bone handle. As
this example is made of bronze and highly
ornamental, it is most likely a replica
produced solely for burial with a male.
Recovered from a tomb in Viterbo, the
blade is marked with deep grooves, and the
handle has an angular grip that would not
necessarily prove functional. The scabbard
has similar grooves along the length,
geometric figures framing the hilt, and the
end is decorated with concentric circles
ending in a flat tip, suggesting it was meant
to stand upright on display.

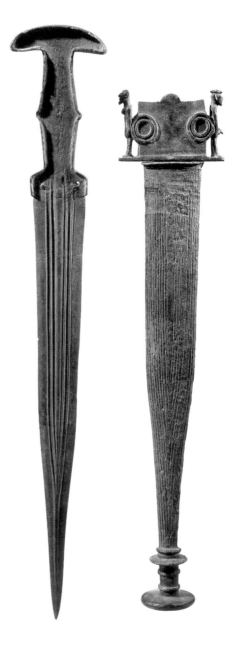

Carved throne

c. 700–650 BCE

Wood • Dimensions: unknown • From Lippi Cemetery, Verucchio, Rimini, Italy

ARCHAEOLOGICAL CIVIC MUSEUM
OF BOLOGNA, ITALY

This intricately carved throne is one of many items found in two tombs excavated in 1972 in Verucchio. The high back of the throne suggests the elevated status of its owner. The carving shows a scene that gives a detailed depiction of textile manufacture. Male and female figures are shown, with men shearing sheep and transporting wool, and women preparing and weaving the wool into cloth. The ornately carved wooden items found in the two tombs, which included thrones, footstools, tables, boxes and bowls, indicate that woodworking was a finely honed craft of the Etruscan people. All were Villanovan in style (known as Geometric in Greece), with intertwined patterns and figures.

MONTELEONE DI SPOLETO CHARIOT

c. 575–550 BCE

Bronze with ivory inlay • Height: 1.3 m (4¼ ft), length 2.1 m (6¾ ft)
• From Colle del Capitano, Monteleone di Spoleto, Perugia, Italy

METROPOLITAN MUSEUM OF ART, NEW YORK CITY, USA

Black figure hydria (water jug) depicting Thetis presenting weaponry to her son Achilles. Although made in Athens, this vase was found in Cerveteri (National Etruscan Museum, Villa Giulia, Rome, c. 550–575 BCE).

There are more than 250 chariots that survive from Etruria, of which this is the most elaborate and best preserved. The detailed decoration, use of new materials such as ivory (both elephant and hippopotamus) and evidence of a new artistic style influenced by imported goods and craftsmen are indicative of the greater affluence seen in grave goods in the 7th and 6th centuries BCE. This chariot was likely used in a ceremonial context on special occasions. Parade chariots, such as this one, were designed to be drawn by two small horses, and had room in the carriage for both a driver and the honouree to stand.

The reliefs depict scenes from the life of the Greek hero Achilles. In the central panel the sea-nymph Thetis presents her son Achilles with armour made by the god Hephaistos. The right panel shows combat between Achilles and Memnon, a scene that is included in Homer's *Iliad*. The left panel depicts the apotheosis of Achilles, riding a chariot similar to the one the scene decorates. The panels illustrate the prevalence of Greek myth in the ancient world.

Biconical urn

9th–8th century BCE

Impasto • Height: 39 cm (15 ¼ in.), diameter: 30 cm (11¾ in.) • From Necropolis of the Osteria, Vulci, Montalto di Castro, Lazio, Italy

VATICAN MUSEUMS, ROME, ITALY

Biconical urns were characteristic of early Villanovan burial practice. Funerary rites included cremation of the body, wrapping the ashes in a cloth and placing them in an urn for burial. The urns were manufactured to have one handle, and evidence suggests that if a functional two-handled urn was to be used for burial, the second handle was broken off. The urns did not have lids but were sealed with a dish or, in the case of male occupants, a replica helmet. Typical of early Villanovan design, this urn is decorated with an incised geometric pattern.

Terracotta hut urn

9th–8th century BCE

Impasto • Height: 27.5 cm (10¾ in.), diameter of roof: 32.9 cm (13 in.), diameter of base: 29.5 cm (11½ in.) • From the area of Albano and Genzano, near Rome, Italy

UNIVERSITY OF PENNSYLVANIA MUSEUM OF ARCHAEOLOGY AND ANTHROPOLOGY, PHILADELPHIA, USA

Hut urns, made of local clay (impasto), are viewed as a reference to the life of the family. In addition to replicating the home, some of the urns contain small household objects such as sets of dishes. The urns closely resemble a typical Iron Age hut – round with a thatched roof supported by beams, sometimes with finial decorations at the apex of the roof or on the ends of the beams. This particular urn was modelled in clay from one piece, with a separate door. The door could be attached with a rope or beam threaded through a loop on the exterior of the door, which slotted into small indentations within the door frame.

Four-wheeled chariot with human figures

c. 710 BCE

Bronze • Dimensions: unknown • From Campi Bisenzio, Tuscany, Italy

NATIONAL ETRUSCAN MUSEUM, VILLA GIULIA, ROME, ITALY

This small cart is an example of an object specifically created for burial. The bowl set into the top would have been used as a brazier for burning incense or other small offerings during the funeral ritual. Unlike carts used by the living, which typically had two wheels, this cart is designed to be free-standing and displayed within the tomb. The figures at the base, between the wheels on all sides, are composed into a series of scenes depicting various activities – hunting, duelling, agricultural work and festivals. These scenes reflect aspects of daily life and are indicative of the values held by the Etruscan aristocracy.

Funeral stela

late 8th–7th century BCE

*Sandstone • Height: 55 cm (21½ in.), width:
25 cm (9¾ in.) • From San Vitale Necropolis,
near Bologna, Italy*

ARCHAEOLOGICAL CIVIC MUSEUM OF
BOLOGNA, ITALY

This roughly rectangular stela, like the
'Zannoni' stela (see page 54), marked
a burial site. The only decoration on
the stone is a depiction of a hut, which
consists of a building with a pitched
roof and two incised squares, which
most likely indicate windows or doors.
Architectural historians find this
illustration of interest for the central pole
and two diagonal support beams holding
the roof, which appears to be the earliest
known representation of this type of
roofing. However, as depictions of the
home were popular in funerary art (as
evidenced by the terracotta hut urn, see
page 45), it is more probable this is simply
an idealized form of hut and not realistic
in its design.

Askos

late 8th century BCE

Impasto • Height: 17.7 cm (7 in.) • From Benacci Necropolis, near Bologna, Italy
ARCHAEOLOGICAL CIVIC MUSEUM OF BOLOGNA, ITALY

A new trend in late 8th-century Villanovan art was to follow the metallurgy tradition of design in clay and combine small statuettes with functional pots. This askos, a small flask for pouring, was found in a grave and is a prime example of this. The askos itself takes the shape of a bull, with the mouth and tail serving as spouts for pouring into or out of the flask. An armed rider, complete with helmet and shield, sits atop a horse on the back of the bull. The simplistic animal forms are decorated with incised geometric motifs.

Votive tablet with Venetic alphabet

6th–5th century BCE
Bronze • Length: 17.5 cm (6¾ in.),
width: 12.5 cm (5 in.) • From Reitia
sanctuary, Este, Veneto, Italy

NATIONAL MUSEUM OF ATESTINO,
ESTE, ITALY

The sanctuary at Este (near modern
Padua) was dedicated to an Italic goddess
called Reitia, a deity of writing. The
sanctuary is known for a large number
of bronze votive offerings that replicate
the instruments of writing such as
styli and tablets. The votives include
writing exercises, magical symbols and
dedications to the goddess. This tablet
is covered with the Venetic alphabet
and a dedication to Reitia. Around
250 Venetic inscriptions are known
from this area of northern Italy. The
offerings left in the sanctuary, in use
from the 6th to the 1st centuries BCE,
were primarily put there by women.

Stylized bronze hands and head

c. 680–670 BCE

Bronze • Height of hands: 23.5 cm (9¼ in.), diameter at wrists: 5.5 cm (2¼ in.) • From the Tomb of the Bronze Chariot, Vulci, Montalto di Castro, Lazio, Italy

NATIONAL ETRUSCAN MUSEUM, VILLA GIULIA, ROME, ITALY

Among a collection of bronze objects found in a small chamber tomb were two sets of hands and this spherical shape on a column with foot, presumed to represent a head. The hands are accurate representations with incised details but the head is undecorated, with no distinguishable features its intended use is difficult to determine. The tomb contained three or four burials and hosted an array of bronze, impasto and other objects. Despite its small size, the deposits in the tomb suggest that the family must have been wealthy.

Zannoni stela

c. 675–650 BCE

Sandstone • Width: 30 cm
(11¾ in.) • From Bologna, Italy

ARCHEOLOGICAL CIVIC
MUSEUM OF BOLOGNA,
ITALY

Stelae were stone slabs commonly used to mark graves, both by Etruscans and other ancient cultures. Typically, the stones were horseshoe in shape and contained two or three registers. This stela is, unfortunately, fragmentary, so while it is possible to see the divide between scenes marked by palmettes at the top, only one register is visible. This depicts, as was common, a journey, probably by the dead to the underworld. Framed by a rope border, one figure can be seen riding a horse-drawn chariot, while the larger figure, on the right, is holding a rein of the horse, perhaps leading or drawing it onwards.

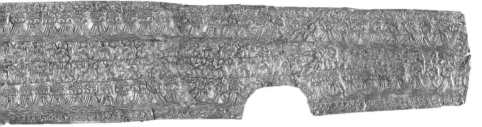

Diadem

c. 650 BCE

Gold • Length: 51 cm (20 in.), width: 6.3 cm (2½ in.), weight: 213 g
(7½ oz) • From Vulci, Montalto di Castro, Lazio, Italy

BRITISH MUSEUM, LONDON, UK

A richly endowed tomb, known as the Isis Tomb, excavated at the
Polledrara Cemetery in Vulci, contained this gold diadem in addition
to a wealth of other luxury items. Named for a bronze statue of Isis,
the tomb probably belonged to an aristocratic husband and wife. Many
of the items, such as a fine gypsum statue, were imported from Egypt.
The gold headpiece shown here is one of the oldest finds in the tomb,
dated nearly 100 years before the other artefacts. It is embossed with a
cable pattern – interlaced semicircles crowned by palmettes – chimeras
and lions. There are semicircular cut-outs so the diadem could fit
over the ears of the wearer.

ETRUSCAN WAGON

c. 650–600 BCE

Wood and bronze • Dimensions: unknown • From Regolini-Galassi Tomb, Caere, Lazio, Italy

GREGORIAN ETRUSCAN MUSEUM, VATICAN MUSEUMS, ROME, ITALY

The Regolini-Galassi Tomb, named for those involved in its excavation, is a two-chambered tumulus tomb that contained a wealth of grave goods. Among these were gold jewelry, silverware, gilded and bronze objects, a chariot (damaged, showing traces of fire that could be from the funeral pyre) and this wooden and bronze wagon. The tomb was found to contain the remains of three individuals: a woman in the end room, a cremated man in the room on the right, and, in an annex chamber, the remains of a third person on a bronze bed. Most of the goods found represent the Villanovan artistic style of the 7th century BCE, including a large fibula decorated with lions and a long bronze plaque depicting animals of Eastern origin.

Including chariots, wagons or carts was a typical burial practice among Etruscans. Carts or wagons, such as this one, were driven from a seated position, unlike chariots, and could be either two- or four-wheeled. Although some found in a burial context show evidence of use in life, many grave inclusions were symbolic, used for the journey to the underworld.

Alabaster cinerary urn showing the deceased (above) and the journey he would make to the underworld in a wagon (below). (Guarnacci Etruscan Museum, Volterra, c. 5th century BCE).

Statue of a winged lion

c. 550 BCE

Nenfro (stone) • *Height: 95.3 cm (37½ in.), length: 73 cm (28¾ in.),*
width: 35 cm (13¾ in.) • *From Vulci, Montalto di Castro, Lazio, Italy*
METROPOLITAN MUSEUM OF ART,
NEW YORK CITY, USA

Made of nenfro, a local volcanic stone used exclusively in
Vulci, this lion is probably one of a pair, the second now lost.
The lion, standing erect, has tightly spiralled wings and,
perhaps surprisingly, bears no trace of paint. Winged hybrid
animals, such as lions and bulls guarding the entrances of
tombs, usually in pairs, are part of a long tradition in funerary
art reaching back to ancient Egypt. In Etruria, statues such
as this were particularly popular for standing guard at the
entrance to the subterranean tumulus tombs. Several similar
nenfro statues of winged lions or sphinxes have been found
in multiple cemeteries across Etruria.

Offering tray

c. 550–500 BCE

Bucchero • Width: 33.7 cm (13¼ in.), depth: 18.1 cm (7 in.) • From Chiusi, Tuscany, Italy

METROPOLITAN MUSEUM OF ART, NEW YORK CITY, USA

Made of bucchero, this offering tray was used in a funerary context, and may represent the larger dining services made of silver or bronze used as part of a banquet. The tray contains a number of small bowls, spoons, spatulas, palettes and other utensils. The tray itself has lions guarding each corner, interspersed with a scroll-like palmette on the sides and rear. Relief figures of a griffin (left) and sphinx (right) are visible on the front panels of the tray. The cut-out in the front of the rectangular tray and perforated base have led some scholars to suggest these trays could be used as braziers.

Pyxis

c. 530–520 BCE

Terracotta • Height (with lid):
15.4 cm (6 in.), diameter: 14.1 cm
(5½ in.) • From a tomb at Narce,
near Civita Castellana, Lazio, Italy

UNIVERSITY OF
PENNSYLVANIA MUSEUM
OF ARCHAEOLOGY
AND ANTHROPOLOGY
PHILADELPHIA, USA

A pyxis, a cylindrical vessel with a lid, was used to hold cosmetics, trinkets or jewelry. This one, made of a fine tan-red clay, sits on three trapezoidal feet, and is painted inside and out. Traces of manufacture remain – the indentation of fingers can be seen in the dark brown paint on the interior. Painted in the geometric style, both the lid and body have alternating bands of patterns including S-shapes and vertical lines. The legs of the box are painted with palmettes and petals, and the feet made to resemble shoes, with criss-crossed lines that may indicate sandals. Tripod pyxides such as this are not common, and it was most likely a rare gift or showpiece of the wealthy woman occupying the tomb.

THE SARCOPHAGUS OF THE SPOUSES

c. 520 BCE

Terracotta • Height: 1 m (3¼ ft), length: 2 m (6½ft) • From Banditaccia
Necropolis, Caere, Lazio, Italy

NATIONAL ETRUSCAN MUSEUM, VILLA GIULIA, ROME, ITALY

Following the popularity of life-sized terracotta statues in Etruria, this husband and wife commissioned a sarcophagus depicting themselves at a banquet. Banqueting was a regular motif in Etruscan art, appearing in wall paintings, on vases and as a subject for funerary items. The sarcophagus was constructed from four large pieces of terracotta, joined together and painted. Another example of a similar monument was found in the same cemetery during excavation, and is now held by the Louvre.

Banqueting in Greece at this time was a strictly male affair; the only women present were slaves or courtesans. The Etruscan practice of husbands and wives dining together was seen as unnatural by the Greeks, leading to a perception that Etruscans were luxurious, frivolous and depraved.

The couple depicted are shown in some detail, propped up on cushions and appear animated through the movement of their arms and hands. The artist focused on their upper bodies, with more emphasis on expression and gesture than on the legs and lower half, which are less articulated, lifeless and somewhat awkward in the position where the torso turns towards the viewer.

Etruscan wall painting of a banqueting scene, depicting a husband and wife sharing a dining couch. From the Tomb of the Shields, Tarquinia, c. 350 BCE. (Ny Carlsberg Glyptotek, Copenhagen, Denmark).

The Republic: Democracy and Expansion

When the Romans expelled the ruling Etruscan kings in 509 BCE, the world changed. Gone were kings, and in their place rose a republic, ruled by Roman men of Roman birth. The creation of the Senate and annual election of a pair of consuls to rule on behalf of the governing body turned Rome into a democracy that they maintained for nearly 500 years with little change.

This new form of government meant there was a need for new artistic expression. Honorific statues were no longer of kings but of ordinary men; large public spaces and buildings were needed to carry out the process of the Republican government. The ruling class of Rome needed a new way to promote, memorialize and commemorate achievement as military leaders and statesmen, and establish a family legacy through portraiture and funerary art.

There were also developments in urban planning, creating cities around the public spaces needed for civic, political and economic life. The Republican period brings in the first real monumentalization of spaces like the Forum in Rome, which in the later years of the Republic would

The Roman Forum became the centre of political, civic, economic and religious life in the Republican period. It became the location of fierce competition among the ruling classes in the later years of the Republic when building was used for self-promotion.

become the focus of increasingly competitive building programmes sponsored by those ruling Rome. Urban planning spread with expansion and colonization, so that other Roman towns and cities came to resemble the capital city, creating an urban landscape that was distinctly Roman, regardless of where it was located.

The expansion of power, first across Italy, then abroad, brought Rome into contact with multiple cultures. Rome had always been marked by inclusiveness of new ideas from the people it conquered, whether it be religion, art or philosophy. The art and architecture of Rome was a blend of native and foreign that became something uniquely Roman. This is particularly evident in the latter half of the Republic. There is a marked difference in Roman art from the late 3rd century BCE when, for the first time, large quantities of Greek art and architecture were brought to Rome after the sack of Syracuse in 212 BCE. The subsequent explosion of Greek art and architecture in Rome had an impact on painting, sculpture and architecture.

The last two centuries of the Republic were marked by an increasing reliance on the public art of rule. Powerful men – both politically and militarily – vied for control of Rome beyond the usual single-year term of a consulship, leading to a proliferation of public art and building that was used to promote and consolidate an individual's power and authority, rather than that of the Senate or the people generally. By the 1st century BCE, men such as Sulla, Pompey and Caesar were using art as a form of propaganda, with such success that the practice was continued throughout the remainder of the Republic and the Empire. The motivation for production and the symbolism contained in public art and architecture are therefore factors worth considering in addition to the object itself.

Art and architecture played a vital role in the competition, perception and machinations of the last leaders of the Republic. The final conflict between Octavian and Mark Antony and Cleopatra in the 30s BCE relied heavily on the use of image and iconography. With the ultimate success of Octavian – who, after 27 BCE, was known as Augustus – promoting ideology and self through public and private art became the purview of the emperor rather than any elected official, changing art again with the change in government.

The sarcophagus of Lucius Cornelius Scipio Barbatus from the Tomb of the Scipios on the Via Appia in Rome. This family tomb, used for 200 years, was a landmark in ancient Rome, and was used to memorialize the achievements of family members and inspire the next generation.

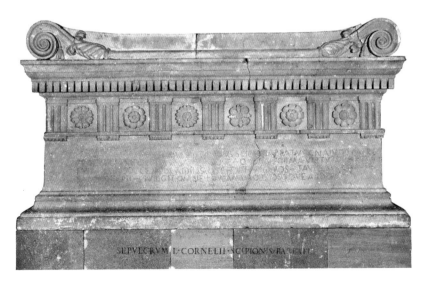

Tripod stand

c. 500–475 BCE

*Bronze • Height: 61.7 cm (24¼ in.), width: 47 cm (18½ in.),
depth: 44 cm (17¼ in.) • From Vulci, Montalto di Castro,
Lazio, Italy*

BRITISH MUSEUM, LONDON, UK

Cast in several pieces then joined, this tripod would
have supported a bowl or brazier. Each leg consists
of three pieces that meet at the top to create arches,
with each arch decorated with a lion devouring its
prey. The tops of the legs feature three pairs of figures,
which have been tentatively identified as Hercules
and Hera, two satyrs, and the Dioskouroi (the twin
brothers Castor and Pollux). The feet of the legs are
also decorated, with claw-footed finials resting on the
backs of frogs, crowned with a diadem of palmettes,
volutes and acorns. The chosen figural groups have no
clear relationship to each other as a motif, yet there
is a similar example in the Metropolitan Museum of
Art. This suggests depiction of unrelated mythological
pairs rather than a comprehensive iconography.

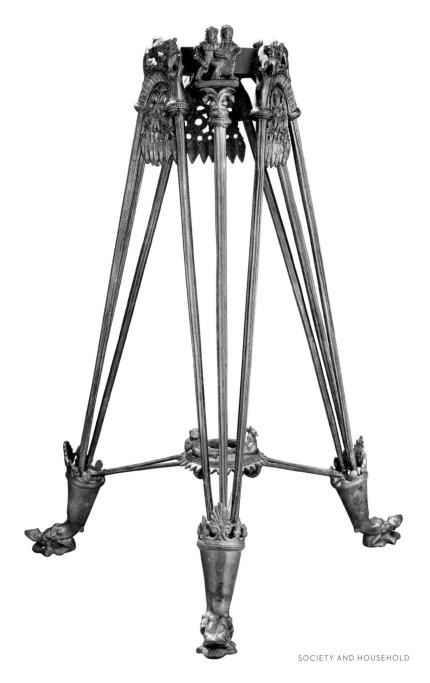

Wine strainer

c. 5th century BCE

Bronze • Length: 30.5 cm (12 in.), diameter: 10.2 cm (4 in.)
• From Vulci, Montalto di Castro, Lazio, Italy

BRITISH MUSEUM, LONDON, UK

This bronze wine strainer is a strictly utilitarian device for
the home, but one that illustrates the importance of wine in
ancient culture. Roman wine, like the modern beverage, varied
in quality and cost. It was, however, of a much stronger alcohol
content, which required mixing with water in order to make
it palatable and to prevent extreme drunkenness. A ritualized
process (particularly at dinner parties or symposia) of mixing
the water and wine in elaborate vessels and pots was inherited
from the Greeks. Wine contained a large amount of sediment,
making strainers such as this one a necessary part of the
process of wine preparation.

Antefix of Medusa

c. 510–500 BCE

*Terracotta • Dimensions: unknown • From Portonaccio Temple, Veii,
near Rome, Italy*

NATIONAL ETRUSCAN MUSEUM, VILLA GIULIA, ROME, ITALY

An antefix was a vertical block covering the edge of a tiled roof, often
carved into a figure or design. This ornately carved and painted antefix
depicts a Gorgon, most likely Medusa. The Gorgons were sisters with
hair of venomous snakes, whose gaze could turn the viewer to stone.
Although two were immortal, Medusa was slain by the Greek hero,
Perseus. Despite their dreadful appearance and reputation, Gorgon
figures were placed on objects and buildings for protection.

Kantharos of a female faun or Io

c. 375–350 BCE
Terracotta • Height: 18.3 cm (7¼ in.),
diameter: 9 cm (3½ in.) • From Apulia, South Italy
LOS ANGELES COUNTY MUSEUM OF ART, USA

This vase is a good example of the melding of two different
artistic traditions into something new. The kantharos,
a deep cup with handles and an indigenous Etruscan form,
is here rendered as an anthropomorphized head, which is a
design of Greek origin. Added to this, it was manufactured
in Apulia, a region in southern Italy that became the centre
of Italian production of Greek-type pottery. The red-figure
decoration at the top depicts a winged figure. That the
head is female is indicated by the pale skin – women were
often painted with creamy white skin on Greek pottery. It
is believed to depict a faun (half human, half goat) or Io, a
priestess of Hera in Greek mythology.

Two women playing knucklebones

c. 330–300 BCE
Terracotta • Height: 21 cm (8¼ in.), width: 22.4 cm (8¾ in.), depth: 12.5 cm (5 in.) • From Capua, near Naples, Italy
BRITISH MUSEUM, LONDON, UK

Made of several separate moulded parts of clay joined together in firing, this small statue group depicts two women playing astragalos (knucklebones). The figures, in a crouched position, are attached to the base by small pegs so that they can be removed. Astragalos was a game of chance using die, most usually made from the knucklebones of sheep. Both board games and those using die were incredibly popular in the ancient world, with depictions of people playing games, and game pieces and markers surviving in the archaeological record (see page 160).

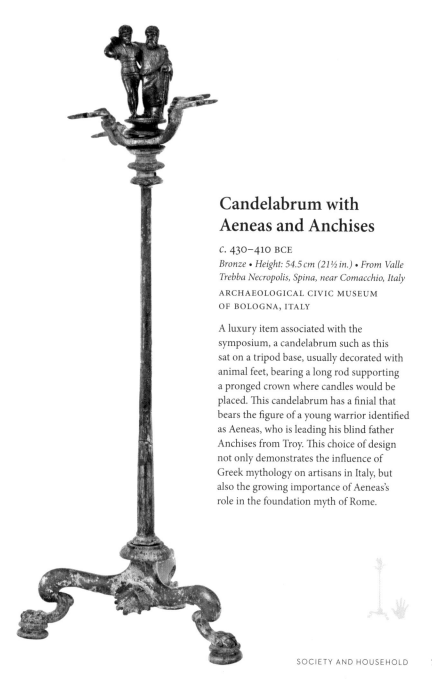

Candelabrum with Aeneas and Anchises

c. 430–410 BCE

Bronze • Height: 54.5 cm (21½ in.) • From Valle Trebba Necropolis, Spina, near Comacchio, Italy

ARCHAEOLOGICAL CIVIC MUSEUM OF BOLOGNA, ITALY

A luxury item associated with the symposium, a candelabrum such as this sat on a tripod base, usually decorated with animal feet, bearing a long rod supporting a pronged crown where candles would be placed. This candelabrum has a finial that bears the figure of a young warrior identified as Aeneas, who is leading his blind father Anchises from Troy. This choice of design not only demonstrates the influence of Greek mythology on artisans in Italy, but also the growing importance of Aeneas's role in the foundation myth of Rome.

Askos of a boar

c. 4th century BCE

Terracotta • Height: 10.5 cm (4 in.) • From Campania, Italy
METROPOLITAN MUSEUM OF ART, NEW YORK CITY, USA

This askos, a vessel used to pour small amounts of liquid such
as oil, is formed in the shape of a small boar. Askoi commonly
came in the form of an animal, whether real or a hybrid of
mythology. This boar, produced in the southern Italian area
of Campania, is made of local reddish-tan clay and covered
in a black glaze slip. A handle is attached to the back of the
animal for ease of use, with spouts at the base of the handle
and from the mouth of the boar. Features of the animal are
quite detailed, including the hooves, small tusks and tufts of
hair around the ears.

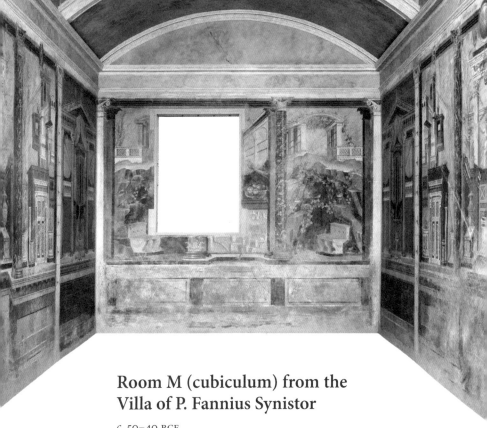

Room M (cubiculum) from the
Villa of P. Fannius Synistor

c. 50–40 BCE

Plaster and paint • Room measures 2.7 x 3.3 x 5.8 m (8¾ x 10¾ x 19 ft)
• From Boscoreale, near Pompeii, Campania, Italy

METROPOLITAN MUSEUM OF ART, NEW YORK CITY, USA

Room M, identified as a bedroom, is decorated in second-style wall
painting. This style, which dominated the 1st century BCE, is based on
a combination of architectural elements and trompe l'oeil. The rear wall
depicts a small grotto with a fountain and statuette of Hekate beneath
a rocky terrain. Framed by two columns, a parapet embellished with a
yellow monochrome landscape supports a glass bowl filled with fruit,
intercut by a window, which looks to be a later addition. The side walls
are divided into four sections by columns, with images of courtyards with
statuary, rotundas, pylons and vegetation alternating with townscapes.

WALL PAINTING FROM ROOM H OF THE VILLA OF P. FANNIUS SYNISTOR

c. 50–40 BCE

Plaster and paint • Height: 1.8 m (6 ft), width: 1.2 m (4 ft) • From Boscoreale, near Pompeii, Campania, Italy

METROPOLITAN MUSEUM OF ART, NEW YORK CITY, USA

This is just one of a series of paintings that decorated Room H, a possible triclinium (dining room) in the villa. The east wall of the room, of which this is the final painting, has a number of Hellenistic scenes, rendered in large-scale painting in the Greek tradition.

Although scholars have been debating the meaning of the paintings since their discovery, general conclusions indicate they may depict a royal wedding or succession to the throne. The first scene shows a woman in purple and white garments, sitting in a chair playing a gold cithara, with a young girl standing behind her. In the central panel, a man and woman sit upon a throne. The male figure is youthful and nude, leaning back in the throne, holding a golden staff. The woman to his right, draped in elaborate robes, leans forward, chin in hand. This stance has led to speculation she is the mother of the male beside her, who is assuming a kingship, rather than a wife. The final panel, pictured here, shows a young woman standing, her gaze turned towards an image of Venus on an opposite wall, resting a gold shield against her leg. There is a figure of a youthful nude male in the centre of the shield. White detailing of a diadem on his head has been used to argue this represents the king from the central panel.

A 1930s model of the villa at Boscoreale, near Pompeii. It is known as the villa of P. Fannius Synistor who was one of its owners in the first half of the 1st century CE. This countryside villa – a variant of the villa rustica – combined luxurious living with agricultural production. The wall paintings in the villa attest to a wealthy owner with exquisite taste.

Mug

c. late 5th–4th century BCE

Terracotta • Height: 6.9 cm (2¾ in.), diameter: 8 cm (3¼ in.)
• From southern Italy

CLEVELAND MUSEUM OF ART, USA

At first glance, there is nothing remarkable about this mug.
It is, in fact, of southern Italian manufacture, but attempting
to mimic the fine bucchero black pottery of Etruscan origin.
Of a simple design, consisting of concentric rings around
the body of the mug, it is the black glaze that produces the
bucchero-like appearance. Slight wearing on the rim and
handle reveals the mug is actually made from a reddish-brown
clay common in southern Italian production, a completely
different hue from the dark greyish-black common in the north.

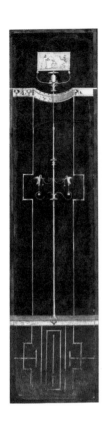

Egyptianizing wall painting

c. 20–10 BCE

Plaster and paint • Height: 2.3 m (7½ ft), width: 0.5 m (1¾ ft) • From Villa of Augustus at Boscotrecase, Naples, Italy

METROPOLITAN MUSEUM OF ART, NEW YORK CITY, USA

Third-style painting, also known as ornate style, was becoming popular when the villa at Boscotrecase was built by Marcus Agrippa, son-in-law and general to Augustus. Most of the rooms are decorated in Second style, but this one, known as the Black Room, is in the newer style. This Third style, like the Second, made use of architectural features, but elongated and embellished them in a manner that was unrealistic. Two-thirds of the wall is black, with a deep red register at the bottom. Golden candelabra support a panel with an Egyptianizing scene of Apis. Swans, a symbol of Apollo, also feature as a recurring image in the room.

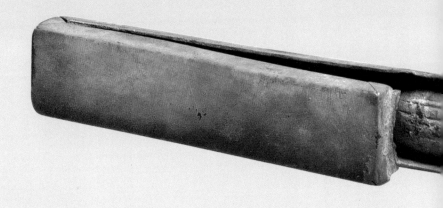

STRIGIL

c. 50–40 BCE

Bronze • Length: 21 cm (8¼ in.) • Provenance unknown
METROPOLITAN MUSEUM OF ART, NEW YORK CITY, USA

A strigil is a curved, cleaning instrument used by both Greeks and Romans, but primarily men only and male athletes in particular. Communal exercise and bathing were typically a daily ritual in the ancient world, often taking hours, and were seen as a social event. Thermae (bathhouses) were large public buildings that included a series of rooms, courtyards and exercise areas. Upon entering the bathhouse, one would have the body rubbed with oil before proceeding to the palaestra (yard) to exercise. This could include weightlifting, athletics, ball games or swimming. After exercise or a visit to the hot room, the body was rubbed with olive oil and the strigil applied to the skin, scraping off the oil, dirt and perspiration before bathing.

Larger public bathhouses (particularly in imperial Rome and other big cities) also held libraries, eateries and gardens, and were more like a modern-day spa than simply a functional place to wash. It is estimated that the Baths of Caracalla in Rome (3rd century CE) could serve 1,600 people at once. Women also attended the baths, but separate from men. They were not expected to exercise in the same manner as men, so their areas often contained smaller open spaces.

Strigils were common everyday objects and, although functional, some were decorated, made of glass or even covered with gold gilt. This one, like the majority of strigils, is made of bronze. It also has the name of the owner, a man named Agemachos, inscribed on the handle.

The Stabian Baths in Pompeii (2nd century BCE), which had separate exercise and bathing areas for men and women. The palaestra used by men for exercise forms the central space of the bath complex.

Scarab ring with archer

late 5th century BCE

*Gold and carnelian • Length of scarab:
1.5 cm (½ in.) • From Etruria, Italy*

J. PAUL GETTY MUSEUM,
LOS ANGELES, USA

Although made and recovered in Etruria, this ring
is Greek in style, and was probably made by a Greek
artist working locally. The scarab ring is an eastern
style, with the image of the beetle (on the reverse)
and an archer on the face of the carnelian stone
made in intaglio. The archer is kneeling and drawing
a bow. There is some speculation this might be a
depiction of Odysseus. The band of the ring is made
of gold, with the prongs holding the stone carved into
the shape of lions' heads.

The Chimera of Arezzo

c. 400 BCE

Bronze • Length: 1.3 m (4¼ ft)• From Arezzo, Tuscany, Italy
NATIONAL ARCHAEOLOGICAL MUSEUM OF
FLORENCE, ITALY

The chimera is a mythical, hybrid, fire-breathing beast typically depicted with a lion's head, a goat rising from its back and a tail with a snake's head. This bronze statue, meant to be viewed in the round, is one of the best examples of the creature. Marks along the flank of the body indicate the animal is wounded, which, combined with the roaring mouth, bristling mane and arched back, suggests it should be seen in combat. Also a votive, it bears an inscription that reads 'tinscvil', meaning 'Offering belonging to Tinia', an Etruscan sky god.

Vessel ornament of
a reclining lyre player

c. 400–375 BCE
Bronze • Height: 5.2 cm (2 in.) • From Italy
CLEVELAND MUSEUM OF ART, USA

A small bronze statuette with traces of gilding,
this ornament depicts a figure reclining on a couch
supported by pillows, holding a lyre. One of six
ornaments, the others represent a flute player,
a figure holding an omphalos (religious stone
artefact) and diners at a banquet. As a group, the
figures illustrate a symposium or banquet, which
was a huge part of social life among Greeks,
Etruscans and Romans. Whether these vessels were
used as functional or decorative items is unknown.

Etruscan gem ring with Hercules at rest

c. 4th century BCE

Gold and carnelian • Height: 1 cm (½ in.), width: 2.5 cm (1 in.), depth: 2.5 cm (1 in.) • From Etruria, Italy

WALTERS ART MUSEUM, BALTIMORE, USA

A well-known type of decoration is incised into the carnelian stone, showing Hercules at rest. His habitually worn lion skin is visible on his back, behind his leg and trailing on the ground, and one hand is holding his club. That he is at rest is indicated by the object in his other hand, a kantharos, from which he is drinking wine. Some attempt is made at providing scenery, with faint indications of a tree behind him. Depictions of Hercules reclining first appear in the 6th century BCE, but this particular type was introduced in the 4th century BCE, and was popular in both Greece and Italy.

Fibula

c. 4th–3rd century BCE
Gold • Length: 8 cm (3¼ in.) • From Campania, Italy
CLEVELAND MUSEUM OF ART, USA

Fibulae are purely functional items, similar
in design to a safety pin, used for fastening
garments in the ancient world. Collectively known
by their Roman name, they are found all over
the Mediterranean. Because of their daily use,
they were made in a range of materials and
styles, ranging from simple bronze or iron pins
to delicate gold fibulae encrusted with stones.
This example is a gold leech-shaped pin with
a small crown-like finial at the top. Gold wire
is used to make the hinge and pin.

Engraved hand mirror

c. 325–300 BCE
Bronze • Height: 28.8 cm (11¼ in.), diameter:
13.9 cm (5½ in.) • From Etruria, Italy
LOUVRE, PARIS, FRANCE

Engraved mirrors of this type were a luxury
item for women. The engraved image depicts
Turan (the Etruscan Aphrodite/Venus)
riding a swan, a frequent companion of the
goddess. This scene is framed by a wreath
of laurel leaves. Mythological subjects such
as this were a popular motif for decorating
mirrors both in Greece and Etruria. The
mirror (including the disc and handle) was
cast as a single piece, which terminates in
the shape of a hind.

Gold necklace

c. 350–330 BCE

Gold • Length: 18 cm (7 in.),
height of head pendants: 2 cm
(¾ in.), height of droplets:
2.5 cm (1 in.) • From
Tarentum, Apulia, Italy

BRITISH MUSEUM,
LONDON, UK

This is an elaborate gold necklace of rosettes, lotus palmettes and female head pendants, made of multiple goldsmithing techniques. Fourteen rosettes and eight lotus palmettes survive, with backings of gold wire and double tubes for stringing the necklace. Eight small pendant heads, die-formed from sheet gold, hang from the necklace, alternating with eight large seed-like pendants. The six large female pendant heads wear spiral earrings, a necklace with a central pendant and a stlengis (tiara) in their hair. Two of these have small horns, leading to the conclusion they depict Io, a priestess of Hera who was turned into a cow. Found in the Greek city Tarentum in southern Italy as part of a tomb deposit, it has been suggested the grave was of a priestess of Hera.

Fish plate

c. 340–320 BCE

*Terracotta • Height: 4.6 cm (1¾ in.),
diameter: 13.1 cm (5¼ in.) • From
Apulia, Italy*

BRITISH MUSEUM, LONDON, UK

Some of the finest red-figure pottery of Italian
manufacture comes from Apulia, including this fish
plate. Three perch and three limpets, painted in red
with white highlights, circle a central rosette and
the sides are decorated with a wave pattern, all on a
black background. Although Greek in technique, the
fish plate is an entirely Italic design, and reflects the
importance of fish and seafood in the southern Italian
diet. The plate slopes in towards the centre, creating a
small well for the collection of sauce, a form unknown
in plates from elsewhere in the Mediterranean.

The Vicarello Goblet

late 1st century BCE–early 1st century CE

Silver • Height: 12.2 cm (4¾ in.), width: 7.8 cm (3 in.) • From Aquae Apollinares, Vicarello, Lazio, Italy

CLEVELAND MUSEUM OF ART, USA

This goblet depicts a multi-figure scene at a rustic shrine to the god Priapus. This view of the goblet shows a maenad (an immortal female follower of Dionysus, god of ritual madness) who, like a satyr on the opposite side, is dancing ecstatically. Priapus was a minor fertility god, protector of livestock, fruit plants and gardens, who was known for his disproportionately large phallus. Priapus is represented on the goblet in the form of a stylized boundary marker placed atop a column.

Red-figure stamnos

c. 490–480 BCE

Terracotta • Height: 33.5 cm (13 in.), width: 40 cm (15¾ in.) • From Vulci, Montalto di Castro, Lazio, Italy

UNIVERSITY OF PENNSYLVANIA MUSEUM OF ARCHAEOLOGY AND ANTHROPOLOGY, PHILADELPHIA, USA

This stamnos (a squat vase with high handles used to store liquids) depicts Hercules fighting with the Nemean lion on one side, and Theseus and the Marathonian Bull on the other. Both images relate stories of heroes fighting animals as tasked by the gods. Based on elements of style and technique, the painting is judged to be the work of the Kleophrades Painter. This anonymous painter was known for red-figure work with well-proportioned figures. Although he worked in Athens, a large number of his products were imported to Etruria.

Set of jewelry

c. 475–425 BCE
Gold, glass, rock crystal, agate and
carnelian • Length of necklace: 36 cm
(14 in.) • From Vulci, Montalto di
Castro, Lazio, Italy

METROPOLITAN MUSEUM OF
ART, NEW YORK CITY, USA

This set of jewelry, consisting of pieces made for both
men and women, is one of the richest collections of
grave goods from Etruria. There are ten items in total,
all of gold, some of which are further enhanced with
stones or gems. This includes a gold and glass pendant
necklace, a pair of gold, rock crystal and carnelian
disc earrings, a gold fibula depicting a sphinx, a pair
of plain gold fibulae, a gold straight pin and five rings.
Two of the rings have engraved scarabs that revolve
on a swivel bezel. One is in the style of a lion ring,
but depicts satyrs instead, and is set with a carnelian.
While the owners of the tomb are unknown, they were
clearly very wealthy.

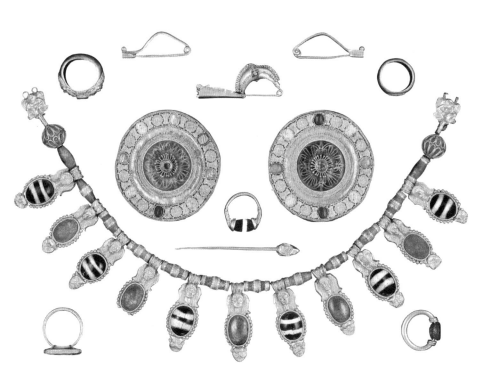

The Boxer of the Quirinal

c. 331–323 BCE
Bronze • Height: 1.4 m (4½ ft) • From Rome, Italy
NATIONAL ROMAN MUSEUM, PALAZZO
MASSIMO ALLE TERME, ROME, ITALY

This Hellenistic bronze statue of a boxer was excavated near the Baths of Constantine in the 19th century, where it was likely on display in antiquity. Seated, the detail of his gloves and wounds suggest he is resting after a match. Copper inlays in the body of the statue indicate blood, which can be seen dripping down his right arm and leg, his right eye is swollen, he has cauliflower ears, his nose is broken and his lips are sunken and scarred, possibly signifying missing teeth. His size and musculature demonstrate the power of his athleticism, a quality venerated in antiquity, as signs of wear on his foot and hands suggest the statue was frequently touched.

Frog guttus

c. 4th century BCE

Terracotta • Height: 5.8 cm (2¼ in.), width: 11.2 cm (4½ in.), length: 9.1 cm (3½ in.) • From Apulia, Italy

CLEVELAND MUSEUM OF ART, USA

Used for sprinkling droplets of liquid during religious rituals, this guttus takes the form of a squat frog. Similar to other vessels of this kind, there is a small handle attached to one side and a spout at either end. Made of local reddish-tan clay, black and white slip have been added to enhance the shape of the guttus. The application of the slip in patterns of stripes and circles makes the depiction of the frog, with bulging eyes and pale underbelly, far more evident than the shape itself indicates.

Cista depicting a Dionysian revel and Perseus with Medusa's head

c. 4th–3rd century BCE

*Bronze • Height: 51.5 cm (20¼ in.), diameter: 26.5 cm
(10½ in.) • From Praeneste (present-day Palestrina),
near Rome, Italy*

WALTERS ART MUSEUM, BALTIMORE, USA

Cista is a general term used to describe a round
or square box used to hold items, typically ones of
value. Most are associated with women's items –
jewelry, cosmetics and mirrors. Numerous examples
of cylindrical bronze cistae sitting on feet like this
one have been found. Typically decorated with
mythological scenes, this example has an all-over
engraved texture of leaves and chains and a handle
made of figures, in addition to scenes of a Dionysian
revel. The fine engravings toward the bottom of the
cista depict Medusa being slain by Perseus, with
the winged horse Pegasus emerging from her head.

Skyphos

c. 1st century BCE

Silver • Height: 9.5 cm (3¾ in.), width: 16.2 cm (6¼ in.), diameter: 10.7 cm (4¼ in.) • From Tivoli, Lazio, Italy

METROPOLITAN MUSEUM OF ART, NEW YORK CITY, USA

A skyphos is a deep two-handled wine-cup on a low flanged base, with ear-shaped handles near the rim. This one, made of silver, has minimal decoration. Patterns of geometric design are located beneath the rim and part of the way down the body of the cup. An interesting feature of the cup is that it is inscribed; on the underside of the foot, the name of the owner – a woman named Sattia – is listed, along with the weight of the cup.

Nile mosaic

C. 100 BCE

Stone • Height: 4.3 m (14 ft.), width: 5.9 m (19¼ ft) • From Sanctuary of Fortuna Primigenia, Palestrina, near Rome, Italy

NATIONAL
ARCHAEOLOGICAL
MUSEUM OF PALESTRINA,
ITALY

The landscape of the Nile depicted in this mosaic is one of the earliest examples of this motif found in Rome. The mosaic, which is curved at the top indicating it was the flooring for an apse in the sanctuary, shows more than twenty different scenes consisting of hunting parties, daily life, ships, mythological creatures, animals, buildings, plants and both Ptolemaic Greeks and black Ethiopians. Some of the scenes are annotated in Greek. Identifiable animals include monkeys, hippopotami, crabs, peacocks, camels, giraffes, lions, lizards, bears, cheetahs and snakes, some of which are not actually native to the Nile region. A somewhat obscure reference in Pliny the Elder's *Natural History* (77–79 CE) indicates that Sulla installed a mosaic floor in the sanctuary at Palestrina, which may be this one.

Laocoön

40–30 BCE
*Marble • Height: 2 m (6½ ft), width: 1.6 m (5¼ ft),
depth: 1.1 m (3½ ft) • From Rome, Italy*
OCTAGONAL COURT, PIO-CLEMENTINO MUSEUM,
VATICAN MUSEUMS, ROME, ITALY

Upon its discovery in the 16th century, this statue was
immediately recognized as one described by Pliny the
Elder that was created by sculptors from Rhodes and
stood in the palace of the emperor Titus (79–81 CE).
This particular arrangement of the subject became
preferred to all other depictions in painting or in bronze.
It shows Laocoön, a priest of Apollo, and his sons,
locked in a struggle with serpents sent by the goddess
Athena. She was angry at him for throwing a spear at
the Trojan Horse, which, although a trick, had been
left by the Greeks at the gates of Troy in her honour.

Copy of Lapis Niger inscription

c. 570–550 BCE
Marble • Height: 61 cm (24 in.) • From the Roman Forum, Rome, Italy

NATIONAL ROMAN MUSEUM, PALAZZO MASSIMO ALLE TERME, ROME, ITALY

A broken piece of black marble in the centre of the Roman Forum preserves the oldest known Latin inscription, of which this is a replica. The original object and surrounding site was venerated throughout antiquity as the burial place of the founder and first king of Rome, Romulus. This is due in part to the word 'rex' (king) in the remains of the fragmentary inscription, as well as early writing that mentioned two large stone lions, such as those used to guard Etruscan tumulus tombs. There is evidence that the area, also containing an altar and enclosed in a white marble fence, was renovated repeatedly during both the Republican and Imperial periods, making exact dating difficult.

Trumpet

c. 400–200 BCE
Bronze • Length: 63.5 cm (25 in.) • From Etruria, Tuscany, Italy
BRITISH MUSEUM, LONDON, UK

This curved bronze trumpet is probably a buccina.
Trumpets such as this, a larger but similarly shaped
cornu or a straight tuba, were commonly used in the
military. Much like in the modern army, trumpets or
horns were used to sound the alarm in battle, to signal
attack, retreat and formation changes during battle,
to announce changes of the watch and were played to
provide accompaniment for soldiers while marching.
In addition to trumpets that survive in archaeological
contexts, there are numerous depictions of this type
of musical instrument being used, such as on
Trajan's Column in Rome.

Etruscan helmet

c. 474 BCE

Bronze • Height: 19.8 cm (7¾ in.), width: 21.7 cm (8½ in.), depth: 24 cm (9½ in.) • From Olympia, Athens, Greece

BRITISH MUSEUM, LONDON, UK

This is a helmet of the Vetulonia Negau type, which dominated from the late 6th until the 4th century BCE. Made from blank sheets of bronze hammered into shape, it was likely produced in Vulci. Proof this helmet was used by a soldier comes from the inscription. Written in Greek, it states: 'Hieron, son of Deinomenes, and the Syracusans, [dedicated] to Zeus Etruscan [spoils] from Cumae'. The helmet was part of the spoils captured after the battle of Cumae in 474 BCE between Etruscans and Syracusans, and subsequently deposited in the sanctuary to Zeus at Olympia.

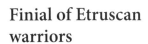

Finial of Etruscan warriors

c. 480–470 BCE
Bronze • Height: 13.3 cm (5¼ in.) • From Vulci, Montalto di Castro, Lazio, Italy
METROPOLITAN MUSEUM OF ART,
NEW YORK CITY, USA

Originally the top of a tall candelabrum, this finial is a good example of early Classical Etruscan metalwork. The figure on the right, an older, bearded soldier, is wearing a complete set of armour, unlike his younger, (unbearded) companion, who has removed his helmet and greaves (leg armour). There is a bandage on the left thigh of the younger warrior, which, together with the way he is being supported by the man on the right, suggests he has been wounded in battle. A lost element of the finial – a spear in the hand of the wounded soldier – is further indication of difficulty walking unsupported.

CURRENCY BAR
(AES SIGNATUM)

c. 280–250 BCE

Cast copper alloy • Height: 9 cm (3½ in.), Length: 18 cm
(7 in.), weight: 1.7 kg (3¾ lb) • From Rome, Lazio, Italy

BRITISH MUSEUM, LONDON, UK

An aes signatum (stamped bronze) is a cast piece of bronze of measured quality and weight used as currency in early Rome. These were stamped – typically with animals of religious significance – by the government in order to prove their legitimacy as currency. It is unclear when the aes signatum was first used in Rome. Tradition has it that this form of currency was introduced by Servius Tullius, the sixth king of Rome, who ruled in the mid 6th century BCE. Generally, however, scholars agree on a mid 5th-century date BCE for their introduction based on the quality of the art with which they are stamped. Aes grave (bronze coinage) was introduced later in the 4th century BCE.

This particular ingot features an elephant on the obverse and a sow on the reverse. The elephant is somewhat unusual, and is helpful in dating the bar. The first elephants seen in Italy were brought by the Greek general and statesman Pyrrhus in 280 BCE when he invaded southern Italy. Sows (or pigs more generally) were commonly used in sacrifice to the gods as part of Roman religion. Mars, the god of war, specifically required the sacrifice of a pig and an ox.

A Roman coin, an aes grave *(heavy bronze), depicting the two-headed god Janus. Minted in 335 BCE, this is one of the earliest Roman coins.*

'Bigio Morata' Portrait of a Nubian

late 2nd century BCE
Marble • Height: 29 cm (11½ in.),
width: 19.5 cm (7¾ in.),
depth: 19 cm (7½ in.) • From Egypt

BROOKLYN MUSEUM OF ART,
NEW YORK CITY, USA

Made of a dark grey marble native to
Anatolia (modern Turkey), this portrait
head of an African man, in a Hellenistic style, was imported to Egypt.
Egypt, under control of Greek rulers since the death of Alexander the
Great in 323 BCE, was becoming increasingly important as a source of
grain for an ever-expanding Rome, and thus was an important centre
of trade. The features of the portrait give clear indication of an ethnicity
other than that of Ptolemaic Egypt, likely representing a Nubian, from
the southern Nile region near modern Sudan. The intricacy of the tightly
curled hair illustrates the exceptional skill of the sculptor. The head was
broken from a larger sculpture near the base of the neck.

Didrachm depicting Romulus, Remus and the She-Wolf

c. 269–266 BCE

Silver • Weight: 7 g (¼ oz)
• From Rome, Italy

BRITISH MUSEUM,
LONDON, UK

Minted in Rome (as indicated by the inscription 'Romano') but of Greek denomination, this silver coin bears, on the reverse, one of the most prevalent images in Roman art. The legendary founder of the city, Romulus, along with his twin brother Remus, were conceived by their mother Rhea Silvia when she was impregnated by a god, typically Mars. Forced to abandon the babies by her brother, who feared a challenge to his authority, they were raised by a she-wolf. The depiction of the wolf suckling them can be found in ancient and modern art, and the image is the symbol for Rome, appearing on public utility works and on the shirts of football club A.S. Roma.

Capitoline Brutus

c. 300 BCE
*Bronze • Height: 69 cm
(27¼ in.) • From Rome, Italy*
CAPITOLINE MUSEUMS,
ROME, ITALY

Undoubtedly of Etruscan production, due to the quality of the metalwork, this portrait of a man combines Hellenistic and Roman styles. It is typical of the realistic style of portraiture prevalent throughout the Republican period. The severe, fixed expression is one that is seen as characteristically Roman. The figure has long been identified as Lucius Junius Brutus, the man responsible for expelling the kings and creating the Republic. This is, however, baseless. The bronze drape at the base is a Renaissance addition, likely from the time it was acquired by the museum. The find-spot is unknown, but this type of portrait bust would have been placed in the home or in a funerary context.

Egadi ram

before 241 BCE

Bronze • Length: 90 cm (35½ in.), maximum height: 67 cm (26¼ in.) • From Egadi Islands, Sicily, Italy

FORMER FLORIO TUNA FACTORY
OF FAVIGNANA, SICILY, ITALY

A number of ships' rams, recovered during the last decade from the sea floor off the Egadi Islands, have changed the understanding of ancient ships and warfare. The size of the rams, attached to the front of the ship and used for puncturing other ships in battle, suggest that ships were smaller than previously believed. Many of the rams recovered from this site have Latin inscriptions, made as part of the casting process, that include important information about officials who ordered their manufacture. One ram has a Punic inscription. The deposit of rams has been identified as the site of the Battle of the Aegates Islands, which took place on 10 March 241 BCE, as part of the First Punic War.

The Lansdowne Throne of Apollo

late 1st century BCE
Marble • Height: 1.5 m (5 ft), width: 0.7 m (2¼ ft), depth: 0.9 m (2¾ ft) • Provenance unknown
LOS ANGELES COUNTY MUSEUM OF ART, USA

A high-backed, elaborately carved marble throne, the Lansdowne Throne is more decorative than functional as a seat. Thought to resemble a throne at the Temple of Apollo at Delphi, the back is carved with symbols of Apollo in high relief: a snake, a bow and a quiver full of arrows. The snake likely refers to the serpent Python, guardian of the oracle at Delphi, which Apollo slew in his youth. Additional decoration includes animal skins draped across the seat, and the base of the legs are carved as the paws of a lion. The original location of the throne is unknown and, as such, so is its purpose.

Coin of Vercingetorix

c. 1st century BCE
Gold • Diameter: 2 cm
(¾ in.) • From Gaul
MUSEUM OF FINE ARTS,
LYONS, FRANCE

This gold coin is one of the best examples of native Gallic currency in circulation in the 1st century BCE. Known primarily from Julius Caesar's own account, *The Gallic Wars*, Vercingetorix became the chief to the tribe of the Arverni in 52 BCE, and is credited with uniting the Gauls against Rome. After successfully defeating the Romans at the Battle of Gergovia, the Gallic forces were defeated by Caesar later in the year. In order to spare the death of thousands of Gallic soldiers, Vercingetorix surrendered himself to Caesar. He was held hostage for five years before being executed on Caesar's orders after being paraded before Rome in a triumph at the end of the wars.

Bust of Julius Caesar (the Chiaramonti Caesar)

c. 30–20 BCE

Marble • Height: 30 cm (11¾ in.) • From Italy
CHIARAMONTI MUSEUM, VATICAN
MUSEUMS, ROME, ITALY

This is one of only two surviving portraits of Julius Caesar that are thought to be true to life. Most likely made after his assassination on the Ides of March in 44 BCE, it depicts Caesar with a stern but wizened visage, typical of the blend of Hellenized and naturalistic portrait style popular in the late Republic. Caesar, already admired by the people before he was killed, was deified and promoted as the saviour of Rome by his nephew and adopted heir Octavian after his death. The pursuit of his murderers by Octavian and Mark Antony kept him in the forefront of Roman politics and memory for decades.

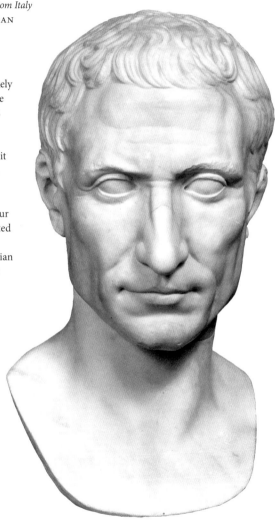

BUST OF HANNIBAL BARCA

c. late 2nd–early 1st century BCE

Marble • Height: 46 cm (18 in.) • From Capua, near Naples, Campania, Italy
NAPLES NATIONAL ARCHAEOLOGICAL MUSEUM, ITALY

After his defeat at the hands of Scipio Africanus in 202 BCE, the Romans destroyed so many images of the Carthaginian general Hannibal that very few depictions of him survive antiquity. This marble bust, likely in the possession of a private citizen, is the only known statue of Hannibal. Depicted as a bearded man with curly hair, this portrait bears some resemblance to the few surviving Punic coins depicting the ruler.

Hannibal is probably best known for his invasion of Italy by crossing the Alps on elephants. His invasion of Italy during the Second Punic War, which lasted nearly fifteen years, resulted in numerous towns and people abandoning Rome in favour of the Carthaginians. His success against Rome at the Battle of Cannae in 216 BCE, in which an estimated 50–70,000 soldiers were killed or captured, led to a massive upswing in Italian support for Hannibal. The city of Capua, the second largest on the Italian peninsula at the time, was one of the territories that joined Hannibal in his war against Rome. The city quickly became Hannibal's base for the remainder of the war. It is probable that this statue was commissioned at that time.

Ruins of houses in Byrsa Hill, Carthage (present-day Tunisia), dating from the 3rd and 2nd centuries BCE. Hannibal Barca launched his invasion of Italy during the Second Punic War from Carthage.

Bust of Cicero

c. 1st century BCE
Marble • Height: 50 cm (19¾ in.) • From Italy
NAPLES NATIONAL ARCHAEOLOGICAL MUSEUM, ITALY

Marcus Tullius Cicero was a politician, lawyer and consul of Rome, and is considered to be one of the finest orators who ever lived. His writings – spanning multiple subjects and genres – make up a large corpus of material that has survived antiquity to inform historians about the last years of the Republic. This statue follows what was a new trend in the 1st century BCE of producing a longer, more stylized bust that included shoulders and the upper part of the torso. Most likely made near the time of his death in 43 BCE, he is depicted as an elder statesman, advanced in years yet dignified, swathed in the many folds of a toga.

Bust of Lucius Cornelius Sulla

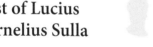

c. 20 BCE
Marble • Height: 42 cm (16½ in.) • From Rome
MUNICH GLYPTOTHEK, GERMANY

A larger-than-life portrait bust, this head has long been attributed to the dictator and general Lucius Cornelius Sulla. Similar in style to a bust of his rival, Marius, the sculptor excelled at rendering the three dimensionality of the face, turn of head and expression. Sulla's face shows some signs of age, but he retains thick, almost unruly hair, which is somewhat rare in Roman portraiture of this period. Made approximately sixty years after his death, there is no other portrait of Sulla surviving antiquity, making it impossible to know if the attribution is correct.

Head of Zeus (Tinia)

c. 425–400 BCE
*Terracotta • Height: 36 cm
(14 in.) • From a temple in
Via San Leonardo, Orvieto, Italy*
CLAUDIO FAINA ETRUSCAN
MUSEUM, ORVIETO, ITALY

This polychrome terracotta head is of a male divinity, most likely the Etruscan god Tinia, who is viewed as an equivalent to Zeus or Jupiter in the Greek and Roman pantheons. Bearing a thick, curly beard with symmetrically distributed, comma-shaped curls, similarly thick, wavy hair parted in the middle and tied at the nape of his neck, and wearing a diadem of laurel leaves, he was painted to have brownish hair and red skin, and traces of white are still visible on the diadem. The head comes from a temple precinct for whom the primary deity is unknown, but is largely assumed to be Tinia.

Statue of Hercules

c. 510–500 BCE
*Terracotta • Height: 1.8 m (6 ft) • From
Portonaccio Temple, Veii, Lazio, Italy*
NATIONAL ETRUSCAN MUSEUM,
VILLA GIULIA, ROME, ITALY

Part of a sculptural group that includes statues of Apollo, Latona and Hermes that stood on the roof of the Etruscan Temple of Apollo near the city of Veii, this life-sized terracotta of Hercules enacts a scene from one of his twelve labours. His third labour, to capture the Ceryneian Hind, sacred to Artemis, resulted in a confrontation between Hercules and the goddess's brother Apollo. Although none of the statues survive entirely intact, Hercules can be identified by the lion skin hanging from his shoulder, visible where it hangs against his left leg.

Statue of Mars

c. 400 BCE
Bronze • Height: 1.4 m (4½ ft)
• From Todi, Perugia, Italy
GREGORIAN ETRUSCAN
MUSEUM, VATICAN
MUSEUMS, ROME, ITALY

This life-sized bronze statue of Mars is exceptional not only for the quality of the metalwork but because it is one of the largest and most elaborate votive offerings that have survived from this period. Missing his helmet and the spear and patera (libation bowl) he once held in his hands, he was dedicated in honour of a god – most likely to the Etruscan god of war, Laran. The dedication of this votive remains; the Umbrian inscription on the skirt says: 'Ahal Trutitis gave [this as a] gift.' The style and pose of Mars indicate the influence of Hellenistic forms of statuary on the sculptor.

Fresco from the Tomb of the Dancers

c. late 5th–mid 4th century BCE

Plaster and paint • Dimensions: unknown • From Ruvo di Puglia, Bari, Italy

NAPLES NATIONAL ARCHAEOLOGICAL MUSEUM, ITALY

The frescoes from the Tomb of the Dancers are the earliest known occurrences of figural wall painting in Apulia. The tomb was constructed by Peucetians, an indigenous Italic tribe. Heavily influenced by Etruscan painting practices, this tomb features six panels depicting approximately thirty women, arms linked, dancing. They are dressed in brightly coloured chitons (draped garments) with veils on their heads, reflective of local textile practices. The skeletal remains of the deceased in the tomb belonged to a warrior, who was dressed in a helmet and greaves and had a shield, spears and daggers in addition to pottery as grave goods.

ZOOMORPHIC RHYTA

c. 430 BCE

Terracotta • Height of ram: 19 cm (7½ in.), width: 9.7 cm (3¾ in.);
Height of mule: 20 cm (7¾ in.), width: 12 cm (4¾ in.) • From Valle
Trebba Necropolis, Spina, near Comacchio, Ferrara, Italy

NATIONAL ARCHAEOLOGICAL MUSEUM OF FERRARA, ITALY

A rhyton is a conical vessel used for pouring or drinking, typically in the shape of an animal's head. The shape was first known in Greece in the Bronze Age, but quickly spread to multiple cultures across Europe and Asia, making it one of the most popular drinking vessels in antiquity. These rhyta, both red-figure, were found in tombs in Valle Trebba, a necropolis in the Etruscan city of Spina. Spina was an important port for the Etruscans, at the end of the Po River on the Adriatic coast, near present-day Venice.

Both are fashioned as animals – a mule and a ram. The mule has its mouth open as if braying, and the neck of the vase is decorated with a dog and silenoi (figures associated with the wine god Dionysus, typically depicted as elderly, white-haired men, with snub noses, balding heads and the ears and tails of asses). The ram's head rhyton also features silenoi, as well as maenads, female associates of Dionysus. That both rhyta feature aspects of Dionysian worship is not unexpected considering the vessels were used exclusively for wine, either at banquets or for pouring libations.

Wall painting of a banqueting scene with a man drinking from a rhyton. Some rhyta had a hole in the bottom of the vessel so that it could be held above the head for pouring wine directly into the mouth (Herculaneum, c. 1st century CE).

Terracotta guttus

c. 4th century BCE

*Terracotta • Height: 8.9 cm (3½ in.),
length: 13 cm (5 in.) • From Campania, Italy*

METROPOLITAN MUSEUM OF ART,
NEW YORK CITY, USA

A guttus is a vessel with a narrow mouth or neck,
from which liquids were poured in drops, typically
used in religious rites and sacrifices. This one is in
the shape of a foot shod in a sandal with a thick
sole. With a small handle attached to the side,
liquid would be poured in through a strainer at the
top of the ankle, and droplets sprinkled out from
a lion-head spout on the rear of the foot. Made of
black-glazed clay, a sandalled foot was a popular
motif for vases in Greek pottery both from Greece
and from southern Italy, such as this example.

Votive uterus

c. 4th century BCE
Terracotta • Length: 9 cm (3½ in.)
• From the sanctuary of Veii,
near Rome, Italy

NATIONAL ARCHAEOLOGICAL
MUSEUM OF FLORENCE, ITALY

This clay model of a female uterus is
a very specific offering dedicated to a
deity in prayer for pregnancy or childbirth.
There are multiple gods and goddesses related to fertility,
childbirth and conception in ancient religious practices, so it
is impossible to know to whom this was dedicated. What is
interesting, however, is the way this is modelled in sections.
It is an attempt at a more realistic anatomical representation
rather than the idealized form typical in the early Hellenistic
period. This may be a reflection of the high degree of medical
knowledge possessed by the Etruscans.

Patera support (Lasa)

c. 3rd or 2nd century BCE
Bronze • Height: 21.6 cm (8½ in.)
• From Etruria, Italy
CLEVELAND MUSEUM OF ART, USA

Lasa is a deity closely associated with
Turan, the Etruscan goddess of love.
This bronze figure of Lasa depicts her in
a typical guise: a winged female, naked
with the exception of jewelry and boots.
She is shown looking into a handheld
mirror and turned to the right, in a
position that is more usually associated
with Hellenistic art. The figure was once
part of a supporting stand for a patera,
a shallow dish used for libations, and a
necessary component of carrying out
sacrificial rites.

Anatomical votive

c. 3rd–1st century BCE

Terracotta • Height: 12.7 cm (5 in.), width: 17.8 cm (7 in.)
• From sanctuary of Veii, near Rome, Italy

BRITISH MUSEUM, LONDON, UK

A model of internal organs rendered in terracotta, this object was a votive offering left for a god or goddess at a sanctuary at Veii. Votive offerings, which could take a variety of forms, were dedicated to a particular deity in exchange for a prayer being answered. Anatomical models such as this one were related to healing, and may have been indicative of the area of the body causing issue. The primary god of healing in the Roman world was Aesculapius, but other female deities such as Juno, Minerva and Diana were also believed to have healing powers.

Tintinnabulum in the form of a phallus

c. 1st century BCE
Bronze • Length: 9.2 cm (3½ in.) • From Rome, Italy
BRITISH MUSEUM, LONDON, UK

Used as bells or wind chimes, tintinnabula were made of bronze and often took the shape of a phallus. Contrary to an association with eroticism, the phallus (specifically the fascinus – the embodiment of the divine phallus) was used as a protective device to ward off evil. These objects often border on the ridiculous, with the addition of wings, hind legs and a tail, as seen here; these were intended to provoke laughter, further enhancing their use as a lucky device by repelling evil spirits. Occasionally, a comically oversized phallus was featured on a figure such as a deity or other personification of protection (see page 93).

Head of Hermes

c. 510–500 BCE

*Terracotta • Height: 40 cm (15¾ in.) • From Portonaccio Temple,
Veii, near Rome, Lazio, Italy*

NATIONAL ETRUSCAN MUSEUM, VILLA GIULIA, ROME, ITALY

The head of Hermes is all that remains of the fourth
statue of the group depicting Hercules's third
labour (see page 123). Hermes, the messenger
of the gods, is depicted wearing a pilos, a
distinctive brimless hat, conical in shape,
that was a common travelling hat in
Illyria and ancient Greece. His
presence at the confrontation
between Apollo and Hercules
is likely down to his attribution
as a god of travelling and border
crossings, as Hercules was tasked
with transporting the hind
from Ceryneia to Mycenae.

Sarcophagus of Seianti Hanunia Tlesnasa

c. 150–140 BCE

Terracotta • Length: 1.8 m (6 ft) • From Chiusi, Tuscany, Italy
BRITISH MUSEUM, LONDON, UK

Found near Chiusi, this sarcophagus is one of a pair probably belonging to the same aristocratic family in Etruria. Made from clay and painted, it features a depiction of its occupant reclining on the lid. An older woman (analysis of the bones contained in the sarcophagus indicate she was around the age of fifty at the time of her death) is leaning on a cushion while she adjusts her mantle with one hand and holds a mirror in the other. She wears a chiton with girdle, a bordered mantle and jewelry comprising a diadem, earrings, necklace, bracelets and finger-rings. The base of the sarcophagus is decorated with columns and rosettes. Her name is inscribed beneath this, in Etruscan.

The Rise of the Empire

The Augustan Prima Porta (Vatican Museums) is one of the most iconic statues of the first emperor of Rome. His breastplate, though military dress, is decorated with scenes of the return of lost standards from Parthia in 20 BCE, an exchange of diplomatic negotiation rather than force.

Augustus revolutionized Rome. He created a new form of government, solidified by the succession of his adopted son, Tiberius, then perpetuated by rulers chosen along familial lines until the death of Nero. By then, in 69 CE, there was no one left who had lived under the Republic, and the change to single rule had become ingrained in the political and cultural mindset of Rome. The change in government changed art. Unlike in the Republic, when different men vied to promote their dedication to Rome and their own images, public art and state art became synonymous. Art and architecture were sponsored and approved (in essence) by one man, resulting in the creation of works that promoted specific ideologies of both the ruler and the state. This included the use of family members, children, heirs and the army. With dynastic rule came dynastic art, creating links to previous emperors through portraiture, iconography and architecture, even when there was no blood tie or when multiple generations had passed. Even centuries later, Augustus was still the model, the emperor to emulate and promote ties to in any way possible.

Ideology was spread through a number of media and by various means. Use of mythology and familial ties to particular deities created the idea of destiny. Portraiture was both Hellenized and veristic – using an individual's features, but in a stylized way that presented youth and strength regardless of one's age or actual physical appearance. Architecture was also used in this way; multiple emperors built their own fora, expanding public space in Rome and promoting their image through mythological ties. Military experience became a necessary aspect of presenting an emperor as a strong leader. Emperors with little to no actual military experience were depicted as generals in statuary. Architecture was also changed by the construction of royal palaces, creating a clear indication of the separateness of the emperors and serving as places that were both public and private, housing great works of art.

The art and architecture of an emperor created a phenomenon of Roman-ness that had not previously existed. Never before had there been a single iconographic and ideological image of Rome, as power and those responsible for public works shifted from year to year. With a programme focused by and on one emperor, a unified approach to art and architecture spread across the Empire. Both public and private art reflected the same images and beliefs, whether it was produced in Rome, Pompeii, Athens or Londinium.

The Empire is often discussed in terms of periods of rule by men classified as 'good' or 'bad' emperors. The transition from one to another sometimes influenced art as well as other aspects of Roman life. The lavish Classicizing style of the last Julio-Claudian, Nero (bad emperor), was countered by the

The Forma Urbis Romae, a large marble map of Rome, was produced and displayed on the side of the Temple of Peace by Septimius Severus in the 3rd century CE. Its accuracy has been verified through archaeological excavation even though only 10 per cent of the original is preserved in the Palazzo dei Conservatori, Rome.

Trajan's Forum, built in 112 CE, was the last of five imperial fora built around the Roman Forum in Rome. In addition to a large open space, it included a basilica, two libraries, a separate dedicated market area and Trajan's Column, decorated with scenes from the Dacian War.

first two Flavians, Vespasian and Titus (good emperors), who returned to a traditional, nearly Republican style of art and architecture. This was abandoned by the third Flavian, Domitian (bad emperor), who returned to a style more in keeping with Nero's tastes. The removal of competition also had an effect on art: the images and names of disgraced emperors could be removed, destroyed or altered. For example, the forum built by Domitian was dedicated and named for Nerva after Domitian's assassination; and Geta, the brother and potential co-ruler of the 3rd-century CE emperor, Caracalla, was physically removed from history by his brother after his death.

As the Empire grew, the art and architecture evolved and changed, with more focus on the provinces, both as sources of influence and as places to build, monumentalize and promote the desired image of the emperor. This only increased with the ascension of emperors of provincial origins such as Trajan (Spain), Hadrian (Spain), Septimius Severus (North Africa) and Severus Alexander (Syria).

Neptune and Amphitrite mosaic

c. 70 CE

Stone • Dimensions: unknown • From House of Neptune and Amphitrite, Herculaneum, Italy

HERCULANEUM ARCHAEOLOGICAL PARK, ERCOLANO, ITALY

On the wall of a small nymphaeum (fountain) in a garden triclinium (dining room) is a mosaic depicting Neptune, the god of the sea, and his wife, the sea-nymph Amphitrite. They stand before a yellow background surrounded by columns with a scallop shell apse above them. The links to the sea are enhanced by the use of shells in the border of the mosaic. The rich colour and small size of the tesserae indicate the wealth of the owners. This is further emphasized by having a purpose-built garden dining room in the house, which is also decorated with mosaics, Fourth-style wall paintings and terracotta theatre masks on an apse featuring a fountain on the adjacent wall.

Coin bank

25–50 CE
Bronze • Height: 12.2 cm (4¾ in.), depth: 13.5 cm (5¼ in.)
• Provenance unknown

J. PAUL GETTY MUSEUM, LOS ANGELES, USA

Money banks, just as we have today, were popular items
in the Roman world, and have often been found buried
with children and young women. Most were simple clay
containers, and not as elaborate or expensive as this object.
Made of bronze with copper inlay forming the decoration
of her tunic, this bank is in the form of a curly-haired,
slightly chubby girl with her arm outstretched.
Whether or not she is meant to depict a beggar
is debatable: her clothes are too fine to suggest
destitution, but the gesture contradicts this. Her
other hand pulls at the top of her tunic, where
there is a slot cut for the depositing of coins.

Carbonized bread

79 CE

*Carbonized bread • Diameter: 21 cm
(8¼ in.) • From House of the Stags,
Herculaneum, Italy*

NAPLES NATIONAL
ARCHAEOLOGICAL
MUSEUM, ITALY

This bread was left in an oven to bake when Vesuvius erupted in 79 CE, forever preserving the loaf as a carbonized relic. Roman bread was typically round in appearance (as here), and made in commercial bakeries on a daily basis. This particular loaf was stamped with the name of the baker: 'Celer, slave of Quintus Granius Verus'. Roman flour varied in quality from very fine to larger grained, depending on what one could afford. This meant the bread also varied in quality, although the same basic recipe was used by all.

Cat footprint on Roman tile

c. 100 CE

Terracotta • Dimensions: unknown • From Gloucester, UK
GLOUCESTER CITY MUSEUM, UK

Despite being in the museum collection since 1969, it was only in 2015 that a museum worker inspecting fragments of Roman tiles discovered the cat's paw. Roman tiles, or tegula, were made from clay and left in the sun to dry, which often led to prints being made by small animals, insects, and even occasionally by people. There are a surprising number of tiles in the collection with prints: dogs, a booted person, a pig and now a cat. The cat walked across the drying tile, leaving traces of three separate prints in the clay.

Lamp in the form
of a comic mask

c. 75–125 CE

Bronze • Height: 12.5 cm (5 in.), width: 6.9 cm (2¾ in.)
• Provenance unknown

J. PAUL GETTY MUSEUM, LOS ANGELES, USA

Theatrical masks, designed in such a way as to
represent identifiable stock characters from Roman
dramas, were popular forms for decoration in the
home. This lamp depicts the 'Leading Slave', a sly and
resourceful trope in comedy, with the typical features
of a scoop-shaped beard, snub nose and furrowed
brow. Curls are mostly hidden by a headscarf, which
is decorated with ivy and berries. Roman lamps were
both functional and decorative items. They burned a
fuel such as olive oil, which was poured in through the
hole in the mouth, with a lit wick emerging from the
spout, and a handle to facilitate carrying the lamp.

Mortarium

1st century CE

*Pottery • Diameter: 29.7 cm (11¾ in.) • From Verulamium
(St Albans), UK*

BRITISH MUSEUM, LONDON, UK

A mortarium is the ancient Roman version of a mortar, used
to grind and mix herbs and spices when cooking. Typically
a round, heavy dish with a pouring spout, it had grit or sand
baked into the clay in order to facilitate grinding. Although
this one was produced locally in Verulamium, the vessel type
was imported to the British Isles before the Roman conquest,
indicating the importance of trade with mainland Europe
prior to the establishment of the province. This dish was
made by a man named Sollus, whose name is stamped on
the rim of the bowl.

Surgical equipment

1st century CE

Bronze and iron • Dimensions: various • From House of the Surgeon, Pompeii, Italy

NAPLES NATIONAL ARCHAEOLOGICAL MUSEUM, ITALY

A typical Italian, atrium-style house, the House of the Surgeon sits in
the northern section of the city of Pompeii in an area known for large
and luxurious homes. It is, in fact, one of the oldest houses in Pompeii,
dating back to the Samnite period in the 3rd century BCE. The house
is named for the collection of bronze and iron surgical instruments
found during excavation. Similar to the medical toolkits used by doctors
until the 19th century, it included scalpels, catheters, probes, forceps
and extractors. Roman medicine, heavily influenced by Greek practice,
was quite well developed for a pre-industrial society.

Carbonized baby cradle

1st century CE

Carbonized wood • Height: 49 cm (19¼ in.), length: 81 cm (31¾ in.),
width: 50 cm (19¾ in.) • From House of Marcus Polius Primigenius
Granianus, Herculaneum, Italy

NAPLES NATIONAL ARCHAEOLOGICAL MUSEUM, ITALY

The eruption of Vesuvius in 79 CE destroyed the cities of Pompeii
and Herculaneum in different ways, which had an impact on
what and how artefacts and buildings survived. Herculaneum, hit
repeatedly by pyroclastic flows of heated, toxic gas, has a larger
amount of preserved organic material than Pompeii, as wood was
instantly carbonized, leaving behind the form of doors, furniture
and other small items. This cradle, instantly recognizable by its
curved runners for rocking and small size, is such an item. It is
a particularly moving piece because excavators also found the
remains of a baby in the cradle, asleep at the time of the eruption.

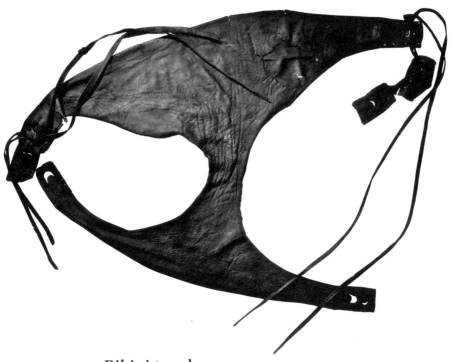

Bikini trunks

c. 43–100 CE
Leather • Length: 34 cm (13¼ in.), width: 22 cm (8¾ in.) • From London, UK
MUSEUM OF LONDON, UK

This pair of leather bikini trunks, small enough in size to have belonged
to a young woman or girl, are one of a number of pairs of similar items
found in domestic Roman rubbish dumps across London. The bikini,
subligaculum, is known to have been worn by women engaged in exercise
or acrobatics. Numerous images of women in such garments have been
found across the Roman world. Famous examples include the statue
of Venus in a bikini from the House of Julia Felix in Pompeii and the
mosaic of the 'bikini girls' from the Villa Romana del Casale in Sicily,
which shows ten women in bikinis engaged in weightlifting, discus
throwing, running and ballgames.

Wall painting of Bacchus and Mount Vesuvius

c. 1st century CE

Plaster and paint • Height: 1.3 m (4¼ ft),
width: 0.9 m (3 ft) • From Pompeii, Italy

NAPLES NATIONAL ARCHAEOLOGICAL
MUSEUM, ITALY

Probably one of the best-known images of Mount
Vesuvius prior to the eruption of the volcano, this wall
painting, from the House of the Centenary in Pompeii,
illustrates the importance of the grape in agriculture
in the region. Bacchus, the god of wine, stands in front
of the mountain, his body covered in grapes and crowned
with a wreath of vines. Vines can be seen growing on the
sides of Vesuvius, whose rich volcanic soil was (and still
is) important for agricultural production. At the bottom
of the painting is a snake and an altar, representing the
lararium, a shrine dedicated to household gods.

Rules of the Library of Pantainos

c. 100 CE

Marble • Height: 42 cm (16½ in.), width: 29 cm (11¼ in.) • From Athens, Greece

MUSEUM OF THE ANCIENT AGORA, ATHENS, GREECE

A local Athenian man by the name of Titus Flavius Pantainos sponsored a library, books and a number of shops around 100 CE. Almost nothing of the library building remains today, but excavators have found part of the dedicatory inscription as well as a plaque stating the rules of the library. Dedicated to the emperor Trajan, the goddess Athena and the people of Athens, the library was open from sunrise to sunset. It was prohibited to remove any of the books from the building ('No book is to be taken out because we have sworn an oath'); in other words, it was a reference library, not a lending library. The building is known to have stood until 267 CE, but what exactly happened to it or its contents thereafter is unknown.

Gladiator helmet

1st century CE

Bronze • Height: 48.3 cm (19 in.) • From Pompeii, Italy
BRITISH MUSEUM, LONDON, UK

Found in the gladiator barracks of Pompeii, this
helmet would have been worn by a retiarius, a
gladiator who fought with the net and trident of
a fisherman. Designed to cover the entire head,
the helmet has a grill of linked circles to cover the
face and a broad brim that protects the side and
back of the head. There is a medallion depicting
Hercules on the front, beneath an angular crest.
The amphitheatre in Pompeii is one of the
oldest in Italy (*c.* 75 BCE), and held
20,000 spectators, far more than the
population of the town. Games
were banned for ten years after a
riot in 59 CE, but had resumed
in the last decade before the
eruption of Vesuvius.

VINDOLANDA WRITING TABLETS

1st to 2nd century CE

Wood and ink • Average length: 18.2 cm (7¼ in.)
• From Vindolanda, Hadrian's Wall, UK

BRITISH MUSEUM, LONDON, UK

To date, more than 700 small wooden tablets containing traces of writing in the form of letters have been discovered at the Roman fort of Vindolanda on Hadrian's Wall. In huge parts of the Empire, letters (and other records) were written on small wooden tablets either covered in wax or using ink. The tablets from Vindolanda are written in ink, whereas the financial records recently excavated from the Bloomberg site in the city of London are the wax variety.

The Vindolanda tablets are remarkable for a number of reasons. They contain a variety of communications – some official, relating to the day-to-day running of the fort, some personal, such as an invitation to a birthday party. They are written by soldiers and by members of their families such as their wives, which illustrates both that soldiers flouted the law regarding marriage and that rates of literacy among soldiers and women were higher than previously thought. Although Roman, these men and women were seldom from Italy but from other provinces in the Empire. They were, however, able to communicate very well in Latin, despite it not necessarily being their native language. As excavations at Vindolanda continue, more tablets are brought to light.

This wall painting from Pompeii, Italy (1st century CE) depicts a series of writing instruments in the lower register. There are a number of styli, ink, a scroll and writing tablets similar to those found at Vindolanda.

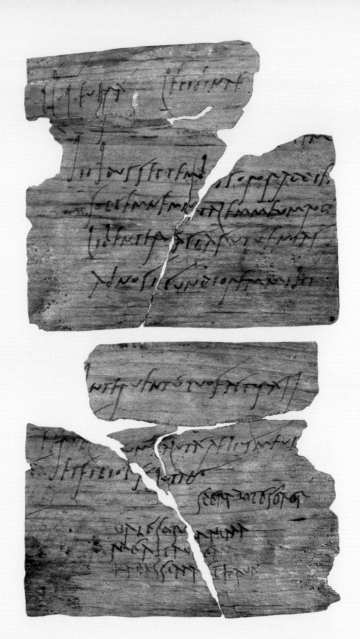

House keys from Cave of Letters

2nd century CE

Wood and iron • Dimensions: unknown • From Cave of Letters, Nahal Hever, Israel

ISRAEL MUSEUM, JERUSALEM, ISRAEL

During the last Jewish revolt against the Roman Empire in 132–136 CE (during the reign of Hadrian), rebel leaders including Bar Kokhba, and others fleeing the advancing Roman Army, took shelter in a cave in the Judean desert. Numerous items were found there, preserved by the arid desert conditions, including letters, household objects and small luxury items such as mirrors and jewelry boxes. Among the items found was this set of house keys, made of iron and bronze. The keys indicate that those who left their homes had secured them, with every intention of returning once the war had ended.

Doll of Crepereia Tryphaena

mid 2nd century CE

Ivory • Height: 29 cm (11¼ in.) • From Rome, Italy

CAPITOLINE MUSEUMS, ROME, ITALY

Found in the coffin of her owner – a girl in her late teens named Crepereia Tryphaena according to her epitaph – this ivory doll was clearly a beloved keepsake. At the time of excavation, archaeologists were touched to find the head of the deceased girl turned to face the doll. Made with joints at the limbs, the doll was poseable, and was probably dressed in a similar fashion to the girl. The doll was found with a small gold ring attached to a key for a box containing grooming tools also found in the sarcophagus. The doll's hair meticulously imitates the hairstyle of the Antonine empress Faustina.

Terra sigillata dish

late 2nd century CE

*Terracotta • Height: 11.2 cm (4½ in.), diameter: 23.4 cm
(9¼ in.) • From Gaul*

METROPOLITAN MUSEUM OF ART, NEW YORK CITY, USA

Terra sigillata (also known as samian ware) is a type of pottery
produced during the Roman Empire with a distinctive glossy-
red finish. The best examples have a mirror-like sheen, and are
believed to have appeared gold in lamplight. Produced primarily
in Gaul and North Africa, terra sigillata comprised both plain,
everyday wares and more expensive versions decorated in relief.
Moulds were used for both versions, creating fairly standardized
shapes, sizes and decoration. This dish has a simple design of
birds and leaves in a repeating pattern with a moulded rim.

Couch and footstool

2nd century CE

Wood, bone and glass • Bench height: 1 m (3¼ ft), width: 0.7 m (2¼ ft), length: 2.1 m (6¾ ft); Footstool height: 0.2 m (¾ ft), width: 0.4 m (1¼ ft), length: 0.6 m (2 ft) • From Rome, Italy

METROPOLITAN MUSEUM OF ART, NEW YORK CITY, USA

Reconstructed from numerous fragments, it is not clear if the elements of this couch and footstool were all originally single objects. As some of the fragments were found near the villa of the emperor Lucius Verus (161–169 CE), it is generally believed to have belonged to his family. The couch legs, similar to other Roman footstools in design, are decorated with friezes of huntsmen, horses and hounds on either side of the Trojan youth Ganymede. According to myth, Ganymede was abducted by Zeus (disguised as an eagle) to serve as his wine steward because of his beauty. The footstool has scenes of winged cupids and leopards. The frame of the couch has lion protomes with glass inlaid eyes.

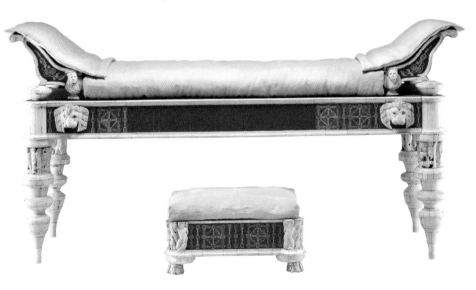

Gaming board

2nd–3rd century CE

Stone, pottery and bone • Board width: 28.5 cm (11¼ in.), length: 31.5 cm (12½ in.) • From Housesteads Roman Fort, Hadrian's Wall, UK

CORBRIDGE ROMAN TOWN, HADRIAN'S WALL, UK

This gaming board, complete with counters, die and a shaker, was likely used to play ludus latrunculorum, a two-player game of strategy similar to chess that is believed to be based on military tactics. Gaming and gambling were popular pastimes in the Roman world, and evidence such as die, small tokens or game boards have been found in multiple contexts. There are some references to the game in ancient texts, but not enough that the rules or methods of the game are fully understood. A number of examples have been found in Roman Britain, demonstrating the popularity of the game among the army.

Circus cup

2nd–3rd century CE
Glass • Height: 9 cm (3½ in.), diameter: 10 cm (4 in.)
• From Varpelev, Denmark

NATIONAL MUSEUM OF DENMARK, COPENHAGEN, DENMARK

'Circus beakers' were mould-blown glass cups decorated with
scenes of chariot racing and other types of games and are
typically found in the western part of the Roman Empire. This
example, found as grave goods in a burial in Denmark, features
painted animals such as a bull, a leopard and a bird. Decorated
with scenes around the entire body of the glass, most circus
beakers featured scenes from the circus with charioteers, often
naming popular individual teams.

The Warren Cup

15 BCE–15 CE

Silver • Height: 11 cm (4¼ in.),
diameter: 11 cm (4¼ in.)
• From Jerusalem, Israel

BRITISH MUSEUM,
LONDON, UK

This silver stemmed drinking cup, which originally had two handles, is of a Hellenistic style but was manufactured in a manner that indicates an Augustan date. It was found in a context with Claudian coins, which suggests it was used through the middle of the 1st century CE. The decoration on the cup is Hellenistic in nature, depicting two scenes of homosexual sex, one between an older bearded man and a younger male youth and one between a young male and a boy. Both scenes are framed by textile hangings and other elements such as musical instruments, wreaths and mantles, suggesting an interior location.

The Great Cameo of France

c. 23 CE
*Sardonyx • Height: 31 cm (12¼ in.), width: 26.5 cm
(10½ in.) • Provenance unknown*

NATIONAL LIBRARY OF FRANCE, PARIS, FRANCE

With twenty-four engraved figures from the Julio-
Claudian dynasty, this cameo, also known as the
Cameo of Tiberius, is the largest to survive antiquity.
Divided into three registers, the upper register depicts
the dead, including the divine Augustus, who is
wearing a crown and holding a sceptre, and Tiberius's
brother and son, both named Drusus. Tiberius,
naked to the waist, sits on a throne in the central
scene, with his mother Livia by his side. Facing him
are Germanicus, his heir, and his wife Agrippina the
Elder. Behind him are future emperors Nero and
Claudius, with Claudius's wife Agrippina the Younger.
The lowest register depicts captured barbarians.

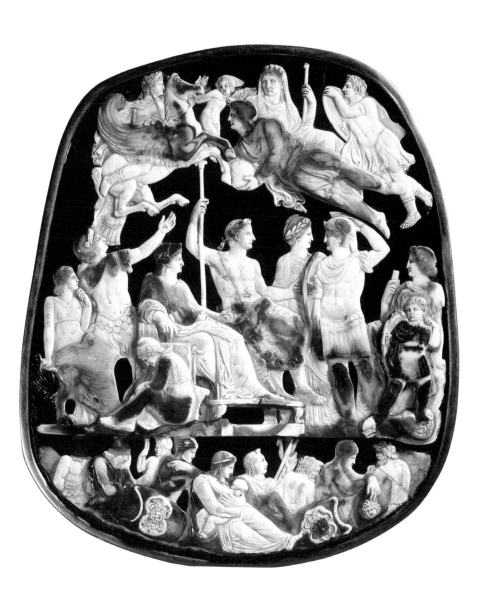

The Portland Vase

c. 1–25 CE

Cameo glass • Diameter: 17.7 cm (7 in.), diameter at rim: 9.3 cm (3½ in.), height: 24.5 cm (9½ in.) • From Rome, Italy

BRITISH MUSEUM, LONDON, UK

This blue-and-white glass vase is considered one of the best examples of cameo glass to survive antiquity. Originally produced in the late 1st century BCE, it was used as a funerary vessel by emperor Alexander Severus in the 3rd century CE. Found near Rome in the 16th century, it came to England to the Dukes of Portland in the 18th century, and has been in the British Museum since the early 19th century. It was famously smashed by a drunkard visiting the galleries in 1845, and was then painstakingly restored. The two scenes carved on to the vase are typically thought to be mythological, likely depicting the marriage of the Thessalian king Peleus and the sea-nymph Thetis (mother to Achilles), but have also been interpreted as an historical depiction related to Mark Antony and Augustus.

BEAKER WITH A
THEATRICAL SCENE

c. 50–100 CE

Glass • Height: 14.3 cm (5½ in.), diameter: 8.9 cm (3½ in.)
• From Syria or Palestine

LOS ANGELES COUNTY MUSEUM OF ART, USA

Roman glassmaking developed rapidly from the 1st century BCE, with changes
to manufacture techniques, making glass more readily available. Glassware was
decorated using a variety of methods, including painting. Painted glass, however,
is not a common find, thus making this beaker particularly valuable. As traces of
gilding remain, this was an especially rich item both in antiquity and today.

Although there are differences of opinion as to how exactly the scene depicted on
the vessel should be interpreted, it is agreed to represent a scene from the theatre.
A woman and a youth are at the centre, wearing heavy cloaks and wreaths; they are
looking towards a closed door. Whether this is a symposium or an interaction at a
brothel is contested. An inscription, in Greek, is too fragmentary to give a clearer
idea, but does seem to represent the words exchanged by actors.

Roman theatre featured both comedy and tragedy, but only comedic plays survive.
Although others are known about, the primary sources are plays by Terence and
Plautus, who were writing in the 3rd and 2nd century BCE. Their plays were based
on Greek subjects, and featured a number of recurring stock characters.

*The theatre of Leptis Magna in Libya, originally constructed in the 1st century CE but
renovated multiple times throughout the imperial period, is similar in style to the Theatre
of Marcellus, often a model for Roman theatres, built a few decades earlier in Rome.*

Mosaic floor with Orpheus and animals

c. 150–200 CE

*Glass and stone • 1.9 × 1.9 m
(6¼ × 6¼ ft) • From Saint-Romain-en-Gal, France*

J. PAUL GETTY MUSEUM,
LOS ANGELES, USA

The central panel of a floor mosaic for a room measuring approximately 4.6 × 6.1 m (15 × 20 ft) features Orpheus at the centre, surrounded by animals and figures representing the four seasons. The patterns of the mosaic feature hexagons containing Orpheus and the beasts, set inside a circle inside a square. Orpheus, a figure from Greek mythology, is wearing a Phrygian cap. He is encircled by a bear, two lions, a goat and two cats. Personifications of the four seasons are framed in the corners – summer in the upper left, following clockwise through to autumn in the lower left. The remainder of the floor is designed with black-and-white geometric patterns.

Sistrum musical instrument

1st century CE
Bronze • Height: 27.9 cm (11 in.)
• From Rome, Italy
BRITISH MUSEUM, LONDON, UK

A percussive instrument that was shaken to produce a jangling sound, the sistrum originated in Egypt and was associated with various Eastern cults, especially the worship of Isis. Despite that, this particular example, found near the River Tiber in Rome, is decorated with images that are oddly both Roman and Egyptian in nature. On the top of the loop is the she-wolf, suckling the twins Romulus and Remus. The handle depicts the god of the Nile and an unidentified female figure.

Roman tragic theatre mask

1st–2nd century CE
Terracotta • Height: 21.6 cm (8½ in.) • From Rome, Italy
BRITISH MUSEUM, LONDON, UK

This mask is of a woman with severely arched eyebrows over deep-set eyes, her hair drawn back in lines of plaits tied in the centre of her head. Masks were used in Roman (and Greek) theatre for a variety of reasons. They were large in size, covering the actor's entire head, which helped to amplify the voice and allowed actors to play multiple roles, including females, as their own face was never seen. The masks were designed specifically for tragic or comedic roles, and had exaggerated features so they could easily be discerned by the audience members at the rear of the theatre.

Cosmetic flask

2nd–3rd century CE

Glass • Height: 12.4 cm (4¾ in.) • From Phoenicia
MUSEUM OF FINE ARTS, BOSTON, USA

This blue glass vase, with ribbed sides, small handles and foot, was a typical item for a woman to use for perfumes, make-up or other toiletries. Cosmetics and perfume were common accoutrements of ancient women of all classes, used to lighten skin, define eyes and lips and enhance features generally. Small flasks and containers such as this were used for storage of these items and, in many respects, wouldn't be out of place on a woman's dressing table today. Glass was very often coloured, either pale green or blue, like this small flask.

Staffordshire Moorlands pan

mid 2nd century CE

Copper alloy and enamel • Height: 4.7 cm (1¾ in.),
diameter: 9.4 cm (3¾ in.) • From Staffordshire, UK

BRITISH MUSEUM, LONDON

A trulla, a small round bowl, this dish is made of copper
alloy with a band of Celtic-style decoration consisting of
eight roundels with pairs of intervening triangles. Each
roundel contains a swirling six-armed shape (almost
paisley-like) centred on a three-petal device inlaid with red,
blue, turquoise and yellow-coloured enamel. The handle,
now lost, would probably have been flat and decorated with
similar enamel inlay. Beneath the rim is a Latin inscription
in turquoise enamel. Difficult to decipher because of its lack
of spacing or punctuation, it seems to name four forts along
Hadrian's Wall and possibly includes someone's name.

The Three Graces

2nd century CE

Marble • Height: 1.2 m (4 ft), width: 1 m (3¼ ft) • From Rome, Italy

METROPOLITAN
MUSEUM OF ART,
NEW YORK CITY, USA

The Three Graces, Aglaia (Beauty), Euphrosyne (Mirth) and Thalia (Abundance), were depicted in both Greek and Roman art as three young girls, linking arms, as if dancing. Representatives of fertility and growth, and beauty in the arts, they had their own cults in Greece and the East. Handmaidens to the goddess Aphrodite (Venus), they play an attendant role, gracing festivals and organizing dances in mythology. Their image was so popular it can be found on mirrors, wall paintings, statues, vases and sarcophagi. This statue, one of the earliest objects that depicts the Graces in this manner, is viewed as the model for many other works of art.

Bowl with lotus buds

2nd–3rd century CE

Faience • Height: 5.8 cm (2¼ in.); diameter: 10.6 cm (4¼ in.)
• From Egypt

CLEVELAND MUSEUM OF ART, USA

Egyptian faience, despite looking like blue-glazed pottery, is actually a silica-based quartz material similar to, but more porous than, glass, which could be poured or moulded into shapes. It is distinctive for its bright bluish-green colour. This bowl, decorated around the body with the buds of lotus flowers, was made using a mould, a new technique that was used to produce faience in the Ptolemaic and Roman periods. Blue lotus flowers, symbolizing rebirth in Egyptian culture, were often depicted in Egyptian art, and lend themselves well to the shade of faience. That the bowl appears slightly lopsided suggests that the mould was not level as the compound was hardening.

Meroë Head of Augustus

c. 27–25 BCE

Bronze • Height: 46.2 cm (18¼ in.), width: 26.5 cm (10½ in.), depth: 29.4 cm (11½ in.) • From Egypt

BRITISH MUSEUM, LONDON, UK

Octavian, or Augustus after 27 BCE, rejected the Republican naturalistic style of portraiture in favour of a Hellenistic style, of which this head is a prime example. Unlike previous statesmen, Augustus would appear young in portraiture throughout his long life. This bronze head, with inlaid glass eyes, is all that remains of a full body statue. Characteristic Hellenistic features include the slight turn to the right and the downward set mouth. The central curl of hair in the middle of the forehead features in all Augustan portraits. This statue was probably dedicated to Augustus in Egypt in the decade following his defeat of Antony and Cleopatra at Actium (31 BCE), when he annexed Egypt as a colony of Rome.

Male portrait (possibly Publius Cornelius Scipio Africanus)

c. 10 BCE

Bronze • Height: 46.5 cm (18¼ in.) • From Villa of the Papyri, Herculaneum, Italy

NAPLES NATIONAL ARCHAEOLOGICAL MUSEUM, ITALY

Thought to depict the general responsible for defeating Hannibal in the Second Punic War in 202 BCE, this bronze head was one of a collection of illustrious Romans in the Villa dei Papiri, destroyed by the eruption of Vesuvius in 79 CE. The portrait is distinctive in the use of incised markings to add detail such as hair, eyebrows and lines in the forehead. There are inlaid glass eyes, and the thin-lipped, grim appearance is in keeping with the perceived image of a strong military leader. Publius Cornelius Scipio Africanus was from a long-standing aristocratic family who had been ruling in Rome for more than a century; he was awarded the appellation of Africanus for his defeat of Carthage.

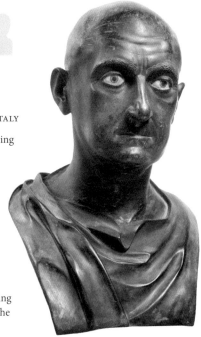

BUST OF LIVIA

c. 31–20 BCE

Basanite • Height: 32 cm (12½ in.) • From Rome, Italy

LOUVRE, PARIS, FRANCE

At first glance, this small, relatively plain portrait bust seems fairly insignificant. It is, however, one of the very first works produced in what became a revolution of ideology and iconography that began with Augustus and continued for centuries. As the emperor was an example for Roman manhood, so his wife was the ideal for Roman women. Probably made soon after the Battle of Actium in 31 BCE, which left Livia's husband in complete control of Rome, this portrait became the benchmark for Roman womanhood for the next forty-five years. Livia was held up as the paragon of a Roman matron: pious, chaste, moral, serving Rome by serving her husband and sons. Livia would be used throughout Augustus's reign, as well as during the reign of her son, Tiberius, as the example all other women should aspire to.

The simple hairstyle, with a nodus (roll) at the forehead, hair pulled back into a tight bun at the nape of her neck and head partially covered with a veil, became the way Roman women were depicted throughout the Augustan Age. Livia was a model not only in comportment, but also in appearance. This trend continued through the years with successive wives of emperors, whose portraiture (specifically, hairstyle) is used to date all female Roman portraits.

The Villa of Livia was just outside Rome and contained a large amount of art, including the famous Augustus of Prima Porta statue of her husband and beautiful wall paintings that replicate a garden (National Roman Museum, Palazzo Massimo alle Terme, Rome).

Praetorians Relief

c. 51–52 CE
Marble • Height: 1.6 m (5¼ ft), width: 1.2 m (4 ft)
• From Rome, Italy

LOUVRE, PARIS, FRANCE

Once part of the Arch of Claudius, built to
commemorate the conquest of Britain, this section
of relief depicts a number of soldiers in great detail.
The three soldiers in the foreground, due to their
oval shields, ceremonial dress and the richness of
their armaments and helmets, have been identified
as Praetorians, a special military unit based in Rome
charged with the protection of the emperor. Three
other soldiers are visible in the background, one of
which is a standard-bearer who does not wear the
same crested helmet. The standard is of the Aquila
type, topped with an eagle holding a lightning bolt.

Sword of Tiberius

c. 15 CE

*Iron, bronze, gilt • Length of blade: 57.5 cm
(22¾ in.), width of blade: 7 cm (2¾ in.),
length of scabbard: 58.5 cm (23 in.), width of
scabbard: 8.7 cm (3½ in.) • From Mainz, Germany*

BRITISH MUSEUM, LONDON, UK

Tiberius, the adopted son of Augustus and
second emperor of Rome, began his career
in the army, successfully leading German
campaigns from 9 to 7 BCE. The blade of the
sword itself is plain and purely functional.
The scabbard, however, made of gilded
bronze, has a number of decorative elements
and an inscription. The uppermost register
depicts a semi-nude Augustus in a pose of
Jupiter, flanked by the gods Mars Ultor and
Victory. Tiberius, in military attire, hands
Augustus a statuette of Victory. The shield
beside Augustus is inscribed to the luck of
Tiberius, and the shield held by Victory is
dedicated to the Augustan victory.

Head of Medusa

37–41 CE
Bronze • Dimensions: unknown • From Lake Nemi, Lazio, Italy
NATIONAL ROMAN MUSEUM, PALAZZO MASSIMO ALLE TERME, ROME, ITALY

Two luxurious ships, more closely resembling floating palaces than boats, were built by the emperor Caligula (Gaius) during his brief reign. Found at the bottom of Lake Nemi about 30 km (18½ miles) from Rome, they were 64–71 m (210–233 ft) long, and decorated with marble, statues, mosaics; they even had bathing suites. This bronze head of Medusa is a protome, a decorative element used as the terminal end of a beam. Other bronzes were also recovered, but they were all in the guise of animals. The ships, preserved and housed in the Nemi museum, were burned at the end of the Second World War by retreating soldiers. Only reconstructions remain today.

Portrait of Vespasian

c. 70 CE
Marble • Height 40 cm (15¾ in.)
• From Naples, Italy
STATE, COPENHAGEN, DENMARK

Vespasian came to power at the end
of the Year of Four Emperors in 69 CE;
he was lauded in Rome for his military
experience as well as his potential to bring
stability to the Empire. Having two grown sons
meant that Vespasian could establish a new dynasty to
replace the Julio-Claudians, who had ruled Rome for nearly a
century before Nero's dramatic suicide. His portrait, done in the
veristic style, reflects his experience and age by representing him
realistically as an older, wiser man. This is a throwback to the
portrait style of the late Republican period, when age and wisdom
were seen as necessary for ruling, and is a dramatic reversal from
the trend begun by Augustus at the end of the 1st century BCE in
which the Julio-Claudian emperors were depicted in a youthful,
idealized style similar to Hellenistic kings.

Boxers' glass

1st century CE

Painted glass • Height: 9 cm (3½ in.), diameter: 10 cm (4 in.)
• From Vindolanda, Hadrian's Wall, UK

VINDOLANDA FORT AND MUSEUM, HADRIAN'S WALL, UK

Similar in technique and design to the circus cup (see page 161), this glass depicts figures of boxers and gladiators. This is hardly an item for everyday use and may seem surprising to find in the context of a fort on the edges of the Empire. It was undoubtedly a luxury item owned by the camp commandant. The theme, one of bouts of combat, is, however, typical for a military installation. Boxing and gladiatorial manoeuvres were used in military training throughout the late Republic and Empire, especially for learning techniques for hand-to-hand combat. This can be seen in the number of arenas and amphitheatres found in association with both forts and veteran settlements.

Trajanic aureus

c. 102–117 CE

Gold • Weight: 7.2 g (¼ oz) • From Rome, Italy
BRITISH MUSEUM, LONDON, UK

This gold coin commemorates the first emperor, Augustus, despite being minted by Trajan nearly a century after his death. The obverse shows the head of Augustus with a laurel crown, and bears the legend 'Divus Augustus', indicating the divine status he was rewarded upon his death. The reverse, showing an eagle between two standards, names Trajan as the commissioner of the coin. The use of Augustus on this coin is an indication of his continued place as the example for all emperors who came after him – he wasn't just the first, he was the best.

Statue of Antinous

c. 130 CE
Marble • Height: 1.8 m (6 ft)
• From Delphi, Greece
DELPHI ARCHAEOLOGICAL
MUSEUM, GREECE

Antinous was a young man from
Bithynia (present-day Turkey) who
became a favourite companion of the
emperor Hadrian during his travels
around the Empire. Killed by an illness
in Egypt, Hadrian mourned his loss,
creating a cult devoted to his memory
and erecting statues to him all over
the Empire. This statue was put up
in the Temple of Apollo at Delphi, of
which the emperor was a benefactor.
As Hadrian was a known Hellenophile,
the statues he commissioned of Antinous
were rendered in Classical Greek style.
Largely intact (only the forearms are
missing), he stands nude, with traces
of a leafy crown in his thick, curly hair.

Equestrian statue of Marcus Aurelius

c. 175 CE
Bronze • Height: 4.2 m (14 ft) • From Rome, Italy
PALAZZO DEI CONSERVATORI MUSEUM,
CAPITOLINE MUSEUMS, ROME, ITALY

This is the only surviving bronze statue of a pre-Christian Roman emperor, due to a case of mistaken identity (as Constantine) in the Middle Ages. It stood on display in Rome until the 1980s when it was moved to the museum for restoration and a replica put in its place. Marcus Aurelius, known as a philosopher and follower of Stoicism, was also a strong military leader, spending the majority of his rule on campaign. This statue, in military garb on horseback, reflects his role as a general and leader. He is considered to be the last of a string of five 'good' emperors whose reigns constitute a Golden Age for Rome.

Severan Tondo

c. 209–211 CE
Wooden panel • Diameter:
30.5 cm (12 in.) • From Egypt
ANTIKENSAMMLUNG,
BERLIN STATE MUSEUMS,
GERMANY

This circular painted panel depicts Emperor Septimus Severus, his wife Julia Domna and their two sons Geta and Caracalla. All are dressed sumptuously, with the emperor and his sons wearing jewel-encrusted gold diadems and holding sceptres. This is probably a type of mass-produced imperial portraiture. What is remarkable is the removal of Geta's face. Geta had ruled jointly with his father and brother from 209 CE, but after their father's death in 211 CE, Caracalla murdered his brother, took sole control as emperor and issued a damnatio memoriae (condemnation of memory), requiring the destruction of his brother's name and image across the Empire.

Planes for woodworking

2nd–3rd century CE

Iron • Dimensions: unknown • From Germany

SAALBURG MUSEUM, GERMANY

Found at the limes fortress near Saalburg, these are the iron remains of woodworking tools that would have been used by soldiers garrisoned there. (Limes marked the fortified frontier between the Empire and its provinces, in this case the Germanic tribal territories.) Originally there were also wood components, forming handles that have not survived. Similar in form to tools used today, the planes and lathes would have been used to cut, trim and smooth wood for construction. The fort itself, as well as the watchtowers and part of the wall that made the limes, were all built of wood, an abundant resource in Germany, and would have required numerous soldiers with the skills necessary to cut and shape the wood.

The Ludovisi Gaul

c. 2nd century CE copy of Greek original
(*c.* 230–220 BCE)

Marble • Height: 2.1 m (7 ft) • From Villa Ludovisi, Rome, Italy
NATIONAL ROMAN MUSEUM, PALAZZO MASSIMO
ALLE TERME, ROME, ITALY

The original work, a Greek sculpture rendered in bronze, was copied into marble and its meaning appropriated by the Romans. The original three-part sculptural group (including *The Dying Gaul,* in the Capitoline Museums and *The Kneeling Gaul* in the Louvre) was produced after the victory of Attalus I over the Galatians (from modern Turkey). Here, the male figure, on the verge of committing suicide, is holding the lifeless body of his wife, whom he has already killed. This is thought to represent a mercy killing, preventing either figure from being captured, killed or violated by the enemy. This motif was used by the Romans to represent Gauls after their defeat by Julius Caesar in the 1st century BCE.

Bust of Commodus as Hercules

c. 192 CE
Marble • Height: 1.3 m (4¼ ft)
• From Horti Lamiani, Rome, Italy
CAPITOLINE MUSEUMS, ROME, ITALY

Commodus, the son of Marcus Aurelius, has a somewhat fantastical reputation due to his appearance in the film *Gladiator*. Although many aspects of the film are grossly incorrect, Commodus did have a reputation for being a licentious and luxury-loving man, who virtually ruined Rome financially, participated in games and fancied himself a god or hero. This portrait, in which he takes on the attributes of Hercules, is a reflection of that. Commodus wears the skin of the Nemean lion, and holds a club and the golden apples of Hesperides as a reminder of the Greek hero's feats. The find-spot of the bust, in an underground chamber in an imperial property on the outskirts of Rome, suggests it was hidden after his assassination.

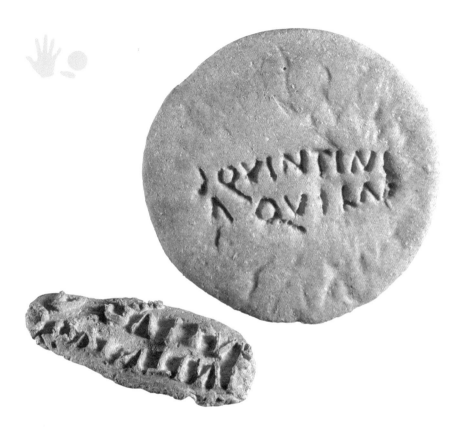

Leaden bread stamp

2nd century CE

Lead • Dimensions: unknown • From Caerleon, Wales, UK

NATIONAL ROMAN LEGION MUSEUM, WALES, UK

Within the army, as in civilian life, bread was a staple food consumed daily, and thus was baked frequently. Within the army, soldiers were responsible for their own food provision to a large extent. As such, it was common for each century (of approximately eighty men) to bake for the group and then use stamps to mark the bread of specific units. This one is stamped for 'Century of Quintinius Aquila' – part of the Second Augustan Legion serving at Caerleon in Wales.

Military diploma

7 March 70 CE

Bronze • Height: 16.2 cm (6½ in.), width: 12.2 cm (4¾ in.)
• From Resina, Herculaneum, Italy

NAPLES NATIONAL ARCHAEOLOGICAL MUSEUM, ITALY

A military diploma (honesta missio) was issued to a soldier when he left the Roman Army after twenty or more years of service. In addition to stating his good standing as a veteran, it granted the right of citizenship and the right to get married. Serving soldiers could not legally marry, although many of them had unofficial wives. The diploma is made of two sheets of bronze, hinged together, and is inscribed on both sides. One side includes the text, the other bears the names of the witnesses to the soldier's discharge. This one, dated 7 March in the second year of Vespasian's reign, grants discharge to a Dalmatian soldier.

Scutum shield

mid 3rd century CE
*Painted wood and hide • Height: 1m
(3¼ ft), width: 0.4 m (1¼ ft) • From
Dura-Europos, near Salhiyé, Syria*

YALE UNIVERSITY ART GALLERY,
NEW HAVEN, USA

A scutum (which actually just
means 'shield' in Latin) is now
identified as a rectangular
semi-cylindrical curved shield that
was used by Roman legionaries.
The only one of its kind to survive,
this type of shield was typically
made of three sheets of wood
glued together and covered with
leather or canvas. It was light
enough to carry with one hand
and covered the centre of the body,
from mid-torso to mid-calf.
A large military fortress was
located at Duro-Europos (modern
Syria) from the 1st through the
4th century CE, when it was
abandoned. An important
archaeological site, the shield
is one of many finds related to
army life in the city.

Ribchester Helmet

c. late 1st–early 2nd century CE

Bronze • Height: 27.6 cm (10¾ in.), weight: 1.3 kg (2¾ lb) • From Ribchester, Lancashire, UK

BRITISH MUSEUM, LONDON, UK

A member of the cavalry used this helmet during games that served as shows of ability and training, not in battle. These often constituted mock battles among elite members of a unit, usually acting out mythological contests between the Greeks and Amazons. Riders and horses would don intricately decorated armour for these matches, such as this helmet, which depicts a battle between cavalry and infantry forces. Held together with a leather strap, the helmet would have been further decorated with a crest box and streamers. A punched-out name appears on the underside of the chin piece – 'Caravi'.

Modius

90–91 CE

Bronze • Height: 28.57 cm (11¼ in.), diameter at base: 30.5 cm (12 in.) • From Carvoran, Hadrian's Wall, UK

CHESTERS ROMAN FORT, HADRIAN'S WALL, UK

A measure for dry goods, most often grain or flour, a standard modius had a capacity of 16 sextarii (just under 9 litres/19 pints). According to the inscription, this one held 17.5 sextarii, but researchers have found it actually holds 20.8, suggesting that someone was being cheated – particularly if this vessel was used to measure grain for payment of tax. Created under the emperor Domitian, its use continued long after his rule. This is indicated by the removal of his name from the first line of the inscription – evidence of the damnatio memoriae issued after his death (see page 192).

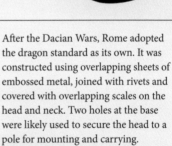

DACIAN DRACO STANDARD

3rd century CE
Bronze • Height: 30 cm (11¾ in.), width: 12 cm (4¾ in.), depth: 12 cm (4¾ in.) • From Niederbieber, Germany

STATE MUSEUM, KOBLENZ, GERMANY

The Dacian Draco was a design of standard originally used by the Dacians, who fought against Roman conquest in two wars in the early 2nd century CE. It consisted of a hollow head of a dragon with open wolf-like jaws containing several metal tongues and a fabric body held up by a pole. When lifted and filled with air, it gave the appearance of movement and made a whistling sound. Marching into battle with the Draco standard and boar-headed trumpets created a visual and audio spectacle undoubtedly meant to terrify the opposing army.

After the Dacian Wars, Rome adopted the dragon standard as its own. It was constructed using overlapping sheets of embossed metal, joined with rivets and covered with overlapping scales on the head and neck. Two holes at the base were likely used to secure the head to a pole for mounting and carrying.

The fort where it was found, at Niederbieber, was a large garrison built around 185 CE to protect the lines in Germany, and probably housed at least one unit of cavalry.

The Germanicus Limes marked the Roman boundary for hundreds of miles, but, unlike Hadrian's Wall, was typically turf or a low stone wall. It was manned by watchtowers and forts, of which there are few remaining traces. Reconstructions of both structures have been built across Germany. This one, at Saalburg, is the most complete reconstructed Roman fort.

Sarmatians paying their taxes on Trajan's Column

106–113 CE

Gesso cast • Height: 1.2 m (4 ft), width: 0.6 m (2 ft)
• From Rome, Italy

MUSEUM OF ROMAN CIVILIZATION, ROME, ITALY

The Sarmatians were a group of people who came from
an area of Asia Minor largely associated with modern
Iran. Neighbours to the Dacians, they were allies in the
wars against Rome in the 2nd century CE. As such, they
appear in multiple scenes on Trajan's Column, which
documents the Dacian Wars fought between 101 and
102 CE, and 105 and 106 CE. In sections spiralling up the
30-m (98-ft) tall column, battles, marches, camp life
and other aspects of a military campaign are depicted.
Included in this are scenes that show the capitulation and
subjugation of former enemies, such as this one, which
shows the Sarmatians paying taxes to Rome in the form
of agricultural goods. Casts of each section of the column
were made in 1861 so that it could be viewed up close.

Funerary inscription for Regina

2nd century CE

Sandstone • Height: 1.1 m (3¾ ft), width: 0.7 m (2¼ ft) • From Arbeia, South Shields, UK

ARBEIA ROMAN FORT AND MUSEUM, SOUTH SHIELDS, UK

At first glance, this appears to be a fairly standard funerary marker, but the inscription reveals that it is evidence of the multicultural nature of the Roman world. The stone was set up by a man named Barates from Palmyra (Syria), in honour of his wife (who was also his former slave), a woman of the tribe of the Catuvellauni, from southern Britain. Found at a Roman fort in South Shields, he had probably come to Britain with the army. Despite her British origin, Regina is depicted as a Roman matron, wearing the clothing of a freeborn Roman woman and with items indicating her role as the female head of a household at her feet.

Statue of Isis

117–138 CE
*Marble • Height: 1.8 m
(6 ft) • From Tivoli, Italy*
CAPITOLINE MUSEUMS,
ROME, ITALY

Found at Hadrian's Villa near Tivoli,
outside Rome, this statue of the
Egyptian goddess Isis was only one
of many Egyptianizing artworks in the
emperor's villa. Despite her Eastern
origin, Isis was popular in the Greco-
Roman world, and temples and statues
dedicated to her can be found fairly
ubiquitously from the 1st century BCE.
She is dressed in a chiton and mantle
knotted in a manner attributed to Isis,
carries an oinochoe (wine jug) and a
sistrum (musical instrument), and her
head is covered with a veil adorned
with the figure of an uraeus (sacred
serpent). Her worship was associated
with motherhood, nature and magic,
and she was popular with both
slaves and citizens.

Neumagen wine ship tombstone

c. 220 CE

Marble • Dimensions: unknown • From Noviomagus Trevirorum (Neumagen), Germany

RHINELAND ARCHAEOLOGICAL MUSEUM, TRIER, GERMANY

This decorative tombstone takes the shape of a Roman warship, complete with a ram, twenty-two oars and a rudder. The stirred-up waves around the ends of the oars indicate the ship is at sea. It is manned by seven men, whose heads are interspersed with a cargo of wine barrels. Interestingly, it was not found near the sea, but in a town on a river. Local historians have taken this to mean this is the oldest wine-producing centre in Germany. It was not uncommon to depict occupations on tombstones, which suggests the commissioner was a wine merchant.

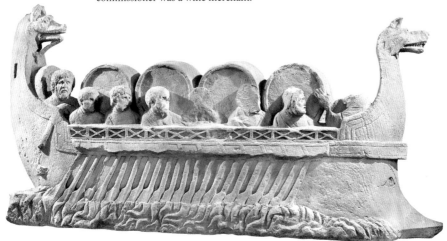

MARBLE STATUE OF THE SUN GOD MITHRAS

2nd century CE

Marble • Height: 1.3 m (4¼ ft), length: 1.4 m (4½ ft) • From Rome, Italy

BRITISH MUSEUM, LONDON, UK

This statue depicts the god Mithras slaying a bull. This is one of three iconic images of the god – the others involve his birth from a rock and a banquet with the god Sol. His garb – trousers and the Phrygian cap – immediately identify him as Eastern. The Romans believed he came from Persia, but his exact origin is unknown.

The worship of Mithras was a mystery cult, which seems to have involved a number of initiation rites but their exact nature is unknown. The god was imported to Rome by soldiers, and he is associated very closely with the Roman Army from the 2nd century CE onwards. Temples dedicated to the god were underground, and featured at their heart a taurocтony, the depiction of Mithras killing a bull, as with this statue. Inscriptions from all over the Empire offer dedications to Mithras or graffiti of lists of members, but provide no further clues as to what following Mithras involved. Surviving inscriptions suggest that only men were permitted to participate in the cult, which may be one reason it was so dominant among the army.

Worship of Mithras took place in an underground temple called a Mithraeum. These could be natural caves or purpose-built, like this one in Capua, Italy (2nd–3rd century CE).

Portrait of a woman, known as 'L'Européenne'

2nd century CE

Painted wood • Height: 42 cm (16½ in.),
width: 24 cm (9½ in.) • From Egypt

LOUVRE, PARIS, FRANCE

Painted on imported cedar wood with traces of gilt, in terms of technique, this is a typical example of a mummy portrait. But her gaze, to the right instead of at the viewer, makes it unique. Wealth is displayed in her clothing and jewels – she is dressed in a purple tunic and yellow cloak fastened with a round brooch set with a large emerald, wears earrings with dark stones set between pearls and has a gold hairpin. This is an example of encaustic painting, using paint combined with beeswax. Gold leaf was added to her necklace and earrings after painting. Made of soft, pliable woods, mummy portraits were sized and shaped to fit the coffin of the deceased.

Votive left foot

2nd–3rd century CE

Bronze • Dimensions: unknown • From London, UK
SCIENCE MUSEUM, LONDON, UK

Votive offerings of body parts were made to healing gods throughout the Empire. These were usually terracotta and the fact that this foot is bronze suggests the dedicator was wealthy. Interesting aspects of this particular votive are the fact that it appears to be wearing a sandal, which oddly resembles a modern flip-flop, and that there is a hole in the base, indicating that it might have been created to hang on the wall of the temple where it was offered. This suggests a permanent display of votive offerings for which there is otherwise little evidence.

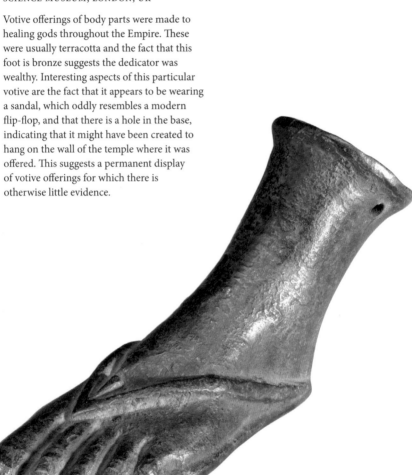

Tombstone of Licinia Amias

late 3rd century CE

Marble • Height: 30 cm (11¾ in.)
Width 33 cm (13 in.) • From Vatican
Necropolis, Vatican City

BATHS OF DIOCLETIAN,
NATIONAL ROMAN MUSEUM,
ROME, ITALY

This fragmentary inscription from the tomb of a woman named Licinia Amias illustrates the momentous changes taking place in Rome in the 3rd century CE. The inscription is not only multilingual, featuring both Greek and Latin, but it also portrays elements of both Roman paganism and Christianity. It begins with the letters 'D M', a dedication to the manes, the Roman gods of the underworld, followed by the Greek ichthus zonton (fish of the living) and a depiction of fish, referencing Christ. Her name and age (lost from the bottom of the stone) are then given in Latin. This illustrates the shift taking place from one religious system to the other, and is representative of a time when both coexisted, with elements of each being practised.

CHILD'S SARCOPHAGUS

3rd century CE

Marble • Height: 0.4 m (1¼ ft.), width: 1.1 m (3½ ft), depth: 0.4 m (1¼ ft) • From Ostia, Italy

BRITISH MUSEUM, LONDON, UK

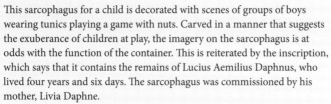

This sarcophagus for a child is decorated with scenes of groups of boys wearing tunics playing a game with nuts. Carved in a manner that suggests the exuberance of children at play, the imagery on the sarcophagus is at odds with the function of the container. This is reiterated by the inscription, which says that it contains the remains of Lucius Aemilius Daphnus, who lived four years and six days. The sarcophagus was commissioned by his mother, Livia Daphne.

Children were not an unusual feature in imperial art, but more often than not they were depicted as little adults, illustrating their potential for when they grew up or as part of a portrayal of dynastic ambitions, especially for the emperor's family. Children were rarely shown behaving as children. Moreover, very young children were, by law, not to be mourned excessively or have expensive burials. This sarcophagus, and many others like it, demonstrate clearly that, despite this, parents grieved and commemorated lost children and that the feeling of personal loss was more important than maintaining a sense of what was viewed as proper Roman behaviour. The inscription shows this as well – it is typically those who are young who have their ages so carefully recorded.

The necropolis of Isola Sacra (Fiumicino, Italy) was used between the 1st and 6th century CE. Most of the tombs were above-ground house tombs with rich decoration, many holding a number of sarcophagi belonging to multiple members of the same family.

The Rise of Christianity, the Fall of Rome

Constantine was in the English city of Eboracum (York) in 306 CE when his father died and he was proclaimed emperor by the army garrisoned there. This modern statue is believed to be located near that spot, just next to where York Minster stands today.

The end of the Severan dynasty in 235 CE led to a period of unprecedented chaos, political, social and economic upheaval, and internal and external wars that marked the end of the 3rd century. The remaining sixty years of this century saw twenty-eight different emperors, all but two of whom were murdered. The pattern was for a general to be proclaimed emperor by his troops, rule for a short time over some portion of the Empire, and then be killed. This had an unsettling impact on every aspect of life, including art. Many of the emperors were not in power long enough to formalize an artistic programme, appearing only on a few coins or in a portrait bust or two.

The end of the 3rd century saw a major shift in the reign of the emperor Diocletian (284–305 CE). He separated military and civilian authority in the provinces, making it easier to manage vast territories and ensuring no one man could gain enough power to raise himself to emperor, thus ending the ongoing political upheaval. He also created the Tetrarchy – rule by four men. He chose a co-ruler in Maximian, then each chose a junior emperor, creating a

This porphyry statue of the Four Tetrarchs, who jointly ruled the Roman Empire from 293–313 CE, was made around 300 CE. Moved from its original location, it was built into the corner of the basilica of San Marco in Venice in the Middle Ages.

system of established succession. This new system of rule changed the focus of the emperor's image from a single man to a group. The stability of the Tetrarchy allowed public art to flourish once again, seeing a number of honorific arches and historical reliefs constructed in Rome and elsewhere. It also marked the first new imperial bathhouse constructed in Rome in more than a century, the Baths of Diocletian. It is believed to be able to serve 3,000 bathers at one time, making it the largest ever built in the city. The sheer size of the complex can still be seen today, in Santa Maria degli Angeli e dei Martiri, a church designed by Michaelangelo in the 16th century and housed within the frigidarium (cold room) of the remains of the bath.

At the beginning of the 4th century, the Tetrarchy was destroyed when the two junior emperors, now in charge, each appointed their sons as the new junior rulers. The reintroduction of hereditary succession led to civil war between Maxentius and Constantine. The eventual success of Constantine, the first Christian emperor, changed Rome forever. Not only did he re-establish sole rule and lead the way to converting the Empire entirely, he also established a new capital in the east, renaming the Greek city of Byzantium after himself, making Constantinople the new centre of the Empire in 330 CE.

In addition to building works in Constantinople, he established another administrative centre in Trier (modern Germany), and assumed control of projects left by Maxentius in Rome, including the Basilica of Constantine. Constantine's buildings and artworks were on a massive scale, even if they were not always entirely original. The Arch of Constantine, for example, still standing today next to the Colosseum in Rome, is largely made up of spolia, pieces of older monuments re-appropriated for a new purpose.

The spread of Christianity throughout the 4th century led to new iconography, and a period marked by the juxtaposition of both pagan and Christian symbols in the same

The increasing threat of invasion from barbarian tribes in the 3rd century CE led the emperor Aurelian to build a new defensive wall for the city of Rome. That the previous city wall had been out of use for three centuries demonstrates the changes taking place in the Empire in later years.

object. The practice of both religions continued almost to the 5th century, when an edict of the emperor Theodosius made paganism illegal (391 CE).

The last 150 years of the (western) Roman Empire, although for the most part politically stable, were subject to growing external threats. Provinces started shrinking, barbarian threats grew and it became increasingly difficult to maintain the Empire's borders. During this time, private art, including fine-worked gold jewelry and decorated silver objects, was buried to ensure safekeeping. These hoards, including coins as well as personal and household items, are found on the edges of the Empire, in provinces that were under threat or being abandoned by the Roman Army.

By the mid 5th century, the various tribal groups threatening Rome succeeded, sacking the city twice. After the second time, in 476 CE, Rome and the west were abandoned, power and territory were consolidated in the east, beginning the transformation into what would eventually become the Byzantine Empire.

ROMAN CURSE TABLETS

2nd–4th century CE

Lead • Dimensions: various • From Bath, UK

ROMAN BATHS MUSEUM, BATH, UK

Approximately 130 defixiones (curse tablets) have been recovered from excavations of the bath complex in the city of Bath. The tablets invoke the goddess Sulis Minerva, an amalgamated deity combining attributes of the Celtic Sulis with the Roman Minerva. She was viewed as a nurturing mother goddess who could also exact revenge.

Curse tablets were a common practice across the Roman Empire. When one perceived a wrong – real, such as theft of a personal item, or perceived, such as a slight or insult – it was possible to ask the gods for retribution against the transgressor. For example, one curse found in Bath requests the thief of two gloves to lose his mind and his eyes. The curse was requested by writing on a small square piece of lead, invoking the god and asking for a specific revenge, which was then folded up, pierced with a nail so that it could not be read by another person and thrown in the sacred spring. The requests were often written in a kind of code, or with letters reversed from right to left. The language of the tablets found in Bath is British-Latin, a colloquial version of Latin only spoken in this province. Two of the tablets are in another language, which may be Celtic, but there is currently no consensus among scholars on this interpretation.

The hot springs in Bath (Aquae Sulis to the Romans) were used by the Celts before Roman conquest, by the Victorians who rebuilt the Roman Baths, and are still used by spas today. Various excavations around the bath complex have revealed a large number of bronze and lead artefacts, including pipes, votive offerings and curse tablets.

Left sock for a child

3rd–4th century CE
Wool • Height: 5.5 cm (2½ in.), length: 12.5 cm (5 in.)
• From Antinoupolis, Egypt

BRITISH MUSEUM, LONDON, UK

This small knit sock made for the left foot of a
child is one of two recovered from a necropolis in
Antinoupolis. This one is made in multiple colours.
The toes, in green wool, are separated, suggesting
that the sock may have been worn with some kind
of sandal with a thong fitting. The knitted socks
found from this period of Egypt are the earliest
known examples of a technique called naalebinding,
which involves the use of a single needle and involves
passing the full length of the working thread through
each loop. This method of textile production predates
both knitting and crochet.

RELIEF DEPICTING MAKING BREAD

c. late 3rd–early 4th century CE

Stone • Dimensions: unknown • From Augusta Treverorum (modern Trier), Germany
RHINELAND ARCHAEOLOGICAL MUSEUM, TRIER, GERMANY

Augusta Treverorum, modern Trier, became home to the emperor Constantine after he took control of the Empire in 306 CE. Although already a Roman settlement, with portions of the city walls dating back to the German campaigns of Marcus Aurelius (161–180 CE), Constantine undertook a number of building projects in the city. In addition to renovating the Porta Nigra, he was responsible for adding a bath complex and basilica to the city. Some of the construction work Constantine did here would later influence his development of Constantinople.

Multiple bas-reliefs of local stone are part of the remnants of Constantine's time in Germany. Many of these illustrate various aspects of daily life and Roman administration. This relief, for example, shows a man working in a bakery, and is not dissimilar in imagery from other depictions of bakeries from ancient Rome, such as the Tomb of Eurysaces in Rome (*c.* 50–20 BCE) or the wall painting from the House of the Baker in Pompeii (*c.* 1st century CE). Bread was one of the primary staples of the Roman diet.

Supplying the city of Rome with grain was a constant concern, leading to the construction of horrea (large warehouses) in the port city of Ostia, Italy. The Horrea of Epagathus and Epaphroditus was built in the 2nd century CE and used for a number of centuries thereafter.

Wall painting containing chi-rho monograph

4th century CE

Plaster • Diameter: 90 cm (35½ in.) • From Lullingstone Roman Villa, Kent, UK
BRITISH MUSEUM, LONDON, UK

This section of wall painting was found in a Romano-British villa originally built in the 1st century CE. The villa showed continuous occupation (with renovation and remodelling) for more than 300 years. In the mid 4th century CE, the occupants of the house converted from paganism to Christianity, and in doing so, created a small room set aside for worship. This was a common practice in a time before widespread construction of churches. The room was decorated with a series of paintings depicting Christian themes, including the chi-rho, used as a monogram to represent Jesus Christ.

Gridiron

4th century CE
Iron • Length: 28.9 cm (11¼ in.) • From Icklingham, Suffolk, UK
BRITISH MUSEUM, LONDON, UK

An ornate gridiron made of iron bars welded together, this is more elaborate than the standard type found in kitchen settings in Pompeii and Herculaneum as well as in other British villa sites. Gridirons typically consist of straight bars attached to legs with a ring handle, but this features two additional bars bent into the shape of the omega. The omega was part of an early Christian symbol, representing the idea that Christ was the first and last, as the letters alpha and omega were the first and last letters of the Greek alphabet.

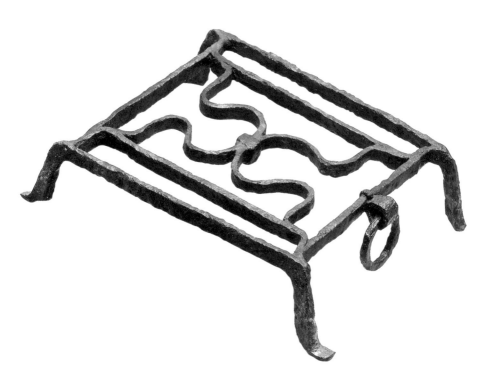

Mosaic panel with a griffin

c. 400–600 CE

Marble • Height: 1.3 m (4¼ ft), width: 1.4 m (4½ ft) • From Syria

J. PAUL GETTY MUSEUM, LOS ANGELES, USA

In addition to guarding treasure or priceless possessions, the mythological creature with the body of a lion and the head and wings of an eagle, known as a griffin, also pulled the chariot of a number of deities. One of these was Nemesis, a goddess associated with retribution against evil deeds and against unwarranted good fortune. In the imperial period, she and her associated griffin became a symbol used to represent the emperor as the maintainer of law and order. This began with Domitian (81–96 CE) and continued through late antiquity. The depiction of the emperor in this guise usually came in the form of a griffin with a spoke (representing the chariot of Nemesis), as can be seen in this mosaic, which was probably once the floor of a villa.

Hoxne pepper pot

350–400 CE
*Silver and gold • Height: 10.3 cm (4 in.),
width: 5.8 cm (2¼ in.) • From Hoxne, Suffolk, UK*
BRITISH MUSEUM, LONDON, UK

An anthropomorphic pepper pot in the shape
of a woman with an elaborate hairstyle popular
in the 4th century CE, this pot is made of two
pieces soldered together. Her hair, clothing
and jewelry are gilded with gold, adding
both detail to her attire and richness to
the piece as a whole. The pot is hollow,
has a serrated bottom edge and turning
mechanisms beneath an opening that
allowed for pepper or another spice to
be put in whole and ground over food.
Due to the design and decoration of the
spice grinder, it is likely that it was made
specifically to be used at the table, not
as a kitchen utensil.

Tunic with Dionysian ornament

c. 5th century CE

Linen and wool • Length: 1.8 m (6 ft), width: 1.4 m (4½ ft) • From Panopolis, Egypt

METROPOLITAN MUSEUM OF ART, NEW YORK CITY, USA

The tunic, a garment worn by women and men throughout antiquity, changed somewhat in style by the late antique period and became more colourful – woven with coloured threads to create patterns. This tunic, despite its 5th-century date, depicts the pagan god Dionysus. The repeating medallions illustrate panthers, bulls and figures such as satyrs and silenoi associated with the god. Dionysus himself is featured in the square plackets on the shoulders of the garment. It is rare for textiles to survive antiquity, and those that have are typically only found in the arid desert climate of Egypt.

Slave collar
with inscription

4th century CE

*Iron and bronze • Diameter of ring: 12 cm
(4¾ in.), height of lamina: 7 cm (2¾ in.),
width of lamina: 5 cm (2 in.) • From Rome, Italy*

BATHS OF DIOCLETIAN, NATIONAL
ROMAN MUSEUM, ROME, ITALY

Although slavery was a huge part of life in
antiquity, marking or collaring slaves was
not very common. There are only forty-five
surviving examples of slave collars, all of
which come from the post-Constantine era
and many (though not all) contain Christian
iconography. They are viewed as punishment
for a slave who had run away. Earlier in antiquity
runaway slaves were tattooed on the face, but this
practice was abhorrent to Christians. This one
is perhaps the best known because of its inscription.
The bronze lamina (the metal plate attached to the collar)
is inscribed: 'I have fled, hold me; when you bring me
back to my master Zoninus you receive a solidus.'
A solidus was a gold coin from the later Roman Empire;
this reward suggests the slave had some value.

Steelyard weight with a bust of a Byzantine empress

c. 400–450 CE
*Copper alloy, lead and bronze • Height: 24.2 cm
(9½ in.), width: 11.5 cm (4½ in.), depth: 7.1 cm
(2¾ in.) • Provenance unknown*

METROPOLITAN MUSEUM OF ART,
NEW YORK CITY, USA

A steelyard balance, used to weigh and move goods,
consisted of a straight beam with a counterweight
at one end that could be moved to balance the load.
Initially developed by the Greeks, this mechanism
continues to be used today. In the late antique period,
the weights used to counterbalance a load often took
the form of an empress. This one, weighing close to
2.3 kg (5 lb), was made of a copper alloy filled with
lead, and had a bronze hook for attaching to the
steelyard. Based on the style of hair and clothing,
it is believed to represent a member of the
Theodosian dynasty (379–457 CE).

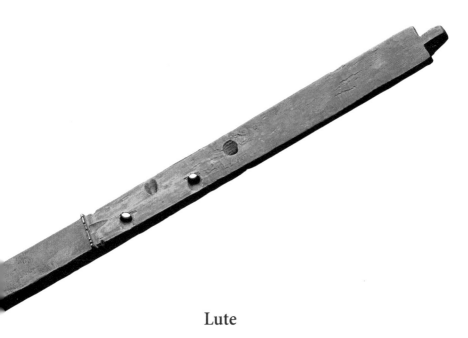

Lute

c. 200–500 CE

Wood • Length: 73.2 cm (28¾ in.), width: 12 cm (4¾ in.), depth: 3.7 cm (1½ in.) • From Egypt

METROPOLITAN MUSEUM OF ART,
NEW YORK CITY, USA

This lute, made of wood with traces of paint, is one of four examples of this type that have survived antiquity. With a long, narrow neck and a sound box shaped by symmetrical indentations (waist), it is thought to be a forerunner of the modern guitar. The lower section of the neck served as a fingerboard and a plectrum was probably used to pluck the strings. Holes on the front of the upper neck once held pegs for four strings, with a now-lost bridge supporting the strings above the sound board. The slightly rounded back of the sound board is made of thin wood perforated by five ornamentally placed clusters of minuscule sound holes.

Medallion with a portrait of Gennadios

c. 250–300 CE

Glass and gold • Diameter: 4.1 cm (1½ in.), depth: 0.6 cm (¼ in.) • From Alexandria, Egypt

METROPOLITAN MUSEUM OF ART, NEW YORK CITY, USA

The image of a youth is made of gold leaf, applied to a disc of dark-blue glass and then covered with a second disc of clear glass, in a sandwiching technique. The bevelled edges of the disc suggest the medallion was meant to be mounted and worn as a pendant. The youth, depicted with thick curly hair, is partly bare-chested with a garment draped over one shoulder. The text, in Greek, says 'Gennadios most accomplished in the musical arts'. This medallion, therefore, was probably an award to celebrate the young man's success in a musical competition.

Handle of a large dish

3rd century CE
Silver and gold • Length: 36.5 cm (14¼ in.)
• Provenance unknown
METROPOLITAN MUSEUM OF ART,
NEW YORK CITY, USA

This elaborately decorated silver handle is all that
remains of what must have been a large serving dish.
The decoration, enhanced with gold gilt, is of a hunting
scene. Centred around a tree, two men on horseback
with spears in hand chase a panther and stags.
Lion, goat and eagle heads also feature as decorative
elements on the edges of the handle, using the shape
of the animals to create a more stylized design of the
handle itself. Hunt scenes were incredibly popular as
a decorative motif, and were one of the few that were
features of both pagan and early Christian art.

Bracelet

late 3rd century CE

*Gold and gemstones • Length: 16.5 cm
(6½ in.) • From Tunis, Tunisia*

BRITISH MUSEUM, LONDON, UK

An incredibly rich item, this heavy gold
bracelet from the Roman Province of
Africa is set with pearls, emeralds and
sapphires. A central roundel of square,
oval and circular bezels is interspersed
with small scrolls. Gemstones are set into
many of the bezels, but many, including
the largest central oval, are empty,
suggesting the stones have been lost. The
openwork ivy-leaf bands that comprise
the armband are set with small pearls,
although quite a few of these are also
missing. The bands were once curved,
but are now flattened. This style is similar
to jewelry of the period from Italy and
other Roman provinces, indicating how
widespread some styles became.

Crossbow fibula

c. 286–309 CE
Gold • Length: 5.4 cm (2¼ in.) • Provenance unknown
METROPOLITAN MUSEUM OF ART,
NEW YORK CITY, USA

This gold crossbow fibula represents a type that became part of
the official insignia of military personnel in the 3rd century CE.
With the arched form of the bow, it more closely resembles the
weapon for which the type is named. This particular fibula bears
an inscription that dates the pin quite precisely. In Latin, it says
'May you always be victorious, Hercules Augustus.' This likely
refers to the Tetrarch Maximian, who liked to style himself as
the Greek demigod. As such, the fibula was probably produced
in an imperial workshop and given as a gift to a military
commander of the imperial house.

Chain with fifty-two pendants

c. 380–425 CE

Gold • Length: 1.8 m (6 ft) • From Romania

KUNSTHISTORISCHES MUSEUM, VIENNA, AUSTRIA

This long cross-body chain would likely have been used for decorating the corpse of a woman for burial. The chain would have crossed over the chest and back by hooking the two loose ends into a ring. The chain, made of small gold loops, has fifty-two pendants of vine leaves and a variety of instruments, such as small knives, forks, spades and other assorted tools. The two sides of the chain are connected through a small gold circle, then joined in a cross-band mount framed by two lions standing on either side of a large smoky quartz. The object was originally thought to belong to a man because of the types of tools depicted, but researchers now believe it belonged to a woman. The necklace is one item of a much larger collection of gold and silver pieces that demonstrate a mixture of Teutonic and Roman techniques and styles, and was likely produced by barbarian goldsmiths influenced by Roman works.

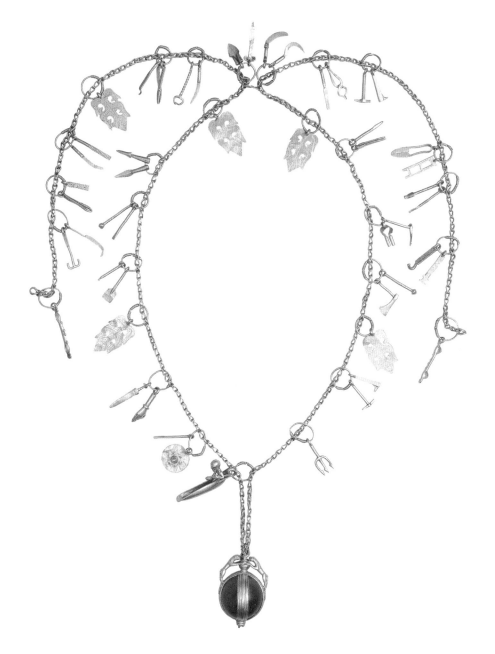

Roman comb

3rd–4th century CE
Ivory • Length: 12.7 cm (5 in.) • Provenance unknown
BRITISH MUSEUM, LONDON, UK

Thought to have come from a tomb, this double-sided ivory comb bears an inscription in Latin. Although the end of the text is debated, the comb belonged to a woman named Modestina. Scholars are unsure if the text reads 'Modestina Vale' (Modestina, farewell), but with the final word misspelled; or if the last four letters are initials, perhaps standing for an expression meaning an admirable and outstanding woman. Combs, as a necessary item, were usually made from bone or wood. Possession of a comb made of ivory (or silver) indicates a higher status for the owner and would have been used not just for grooming but also to decorate the hair once styled.

Plate from the silver treasure of Augusta Raurica

mid 4th century CE
*Silver • Diameter: 53 cm
(20¾ in.) • From Switzerland*
AUGUSTA RAURICA
MUSEUM, NEAR AUGST,
SWITZERLAND

A collection of 270 silver objects was discovered at Augusta Raurica, the site of the oldest Roman colony on the Rhine, founded around 44 BCE. It includes large silver trays, spoons, coins and other objects, including this one decorated with a scene from the *Iliad*. Achilles, dressed in women's clothing to avoid going to war, is discovered by Odysseus. Some of the items were gifts from the emperor Constantine, commemorating the anniversary of his reign. It appears the silver treasure belonged to one or two men, probably high-ranking military commanders. It was buried around 351 CE at the Castrum Rauracense, a nearby fortress built to protect a bridge on the Rhine. This was fortuitous as the fort was sacked by German tribes within a year.

Mildenhall treasure

4th century CE

Silver • Dimensions: various • From Mildenhall, Suffolk, UK

BRITISH MUSEUM, LONDON, UK

The Mildenhall treasure consists of a collection of finely decorated silverware, including two large serving platters, two small decorated serving plates, a deep fluted bowl, a set of four large decorated bowls, two small decorated bowls, two small pedestalled dishes, a deep flanged bowl with a deep, domed cover, five small round ladles with dolphin-shaped handles and eight long-handled spoons. Although few datable coins were included in the hoard, the design and technique of the dishes provide a firm 4th-century CE date. The largest piece (top left) is a massive dish (diameter 60.5 cm/23¾ in.) decorated with scenes depicting the worship of Bacchus.

The Rubens Vase

c. 400 CE

*Agate and gold • Height: 18.6 cm
(7¼ in.), width: 18.5 cm (7¼ in.), depth:
12 cm (4¾ in.) • From Constantinople
(present-day Istanbul), Turkey*

WALTERS ART MUSEUM,
BALTIMORE, USA

Named for the Flemish painter Peter Paul Rubens
who purchased the vase in 1619, this was carved
from a single piece of agate, probably in an imperial
workshop for a Byzantine emperor. Using stone, such
as agate, became increasingly popular towards the
later years of the Empire as it allowed artists to play
with light and colour without using paint. This vase
is covered with intricate weavings of vines and leaves,
and features the face of Pan, a god of nature, music
and shepherds, on either side. The gold rim appears to
have been added in France in the early 19th century.

Corbridge lanx

4th century CE

*Silver • Length: 50.3 cm (19¾ in.),
width: 38 cm (15 in.) • From
Corbridge, Hadrian's Wall, UK*

BRITISH MUSEUM,
LONDON, UK

A lanx was a decorated 'picture platter' intended
for display, not use. This one, found in the bed of
the River Tyne, seems to have been part of a hoard,
as various items were found near the same location
at different times over the last few centuries. As
no major silver-working manufacture was known
in Britain at the time, it was most likely a luxury
imported item. The scene it depicts is one set at a
shrine of the god Apollo. He stands at the entrance
to the shrine with a bow and a lyre at his feet. On
the left, his twin sister Artemis is engaged with the
goddess Athena. Two other unidentified female
figures appear at the centre of the scene.

The Lycurgus Cup

4th century CE

*Silver and glass • Height: 15.9 cm
(6¼ in.), diameter: 13.2 cm
(5¼ in.) • Provenance unknown*

BRITISH MUSEUM, LONDON, UK

This glass cage cup, depicting the death
of the mythical king Lycurgus, is
remarkable both as one of the most
complete and intricately decorated
cups of its kind to survive antiquity
(glass cage cups usually had geometric,
not figural designs) and because it is the
only complete example of a vessel made with dichroic
glass. This glass contains nanoparticles of gold or silver,
and changes colour depending on the lighting. The cup
appears green when lit from the front and changes to
red when lit from behind. Modern glassmakers have
attempted to recreate this technique and have so far been
unable to discern how the Romans made this cup without
the use of laser cutting.

HOXNE TREASURE
BODY CHAIN

5th century CE

Gold • Length: 84 cm (33 in.), weight: 249.5 g (8¾ oz) • From Hoxne, Suffolk, UK

BRITISH MUSEUM, LONDON, UK

Four gold chains of a complex loop-in-loop design are joined to form a body chain worn by passing over the shoulders, under the arms and crossing at both front and back. Every chain terminates in a small lion's head. Joined by rings, the lion heads connect to the mount at both front and back. The front mount has an oval setting for nine gemstones, including an amethyst, garnets and spaces where it is believed pearls once belonged. The rear mount is fashioned using a solidus of Gratian, who was emperor between 367 and 383 CE. The size of the chain suggests it was worn by a slim woman or a young girl.

The emperor Gratian favoured Christianity, at a time when both Christianity and paganism were being followed simultaneously. His refusal to pay tribute to the Divine Emperors and his removal of the Altar of Victory from the Senate marked a clear rejection of traditional Roman religion. Using one of his coins as the centrepiece of this necklace indicates its owner was also a Christian, and was proclaiming so through this necklace. Based on the date of Gratian's death, this would have made the owner an early adherent of Christianity in the British Isles.

The Hoxne Hoard, the richest collection discovered from Roman Britain, included nearly 15,000 coins made of gold, silver and bronze, dating from the late 4th and early 5th century CE. The hoard includes coins minted under the authority of the emperors Constantine II (337–340), Valentinian I (364–375) and Honorius (393–423).

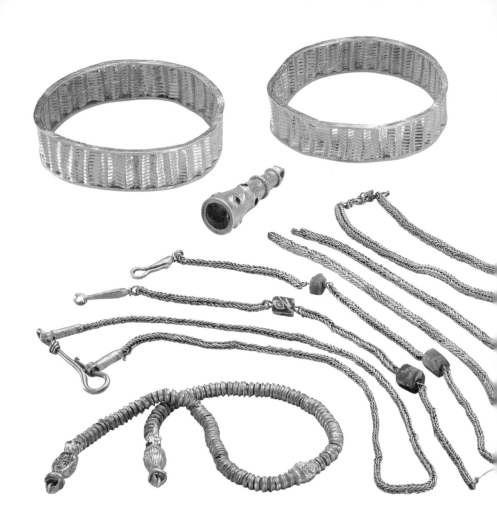

Thetford hoard

4th century CE

Gold • Dimensions: various • From Thetford, Norfolk, UK

BRITISH MUSEUM, LONDON, UK

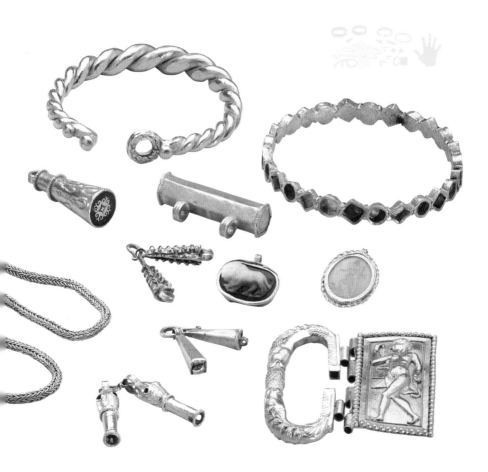

In addition to various silver tableware items like those found in other Romano-British hoards, this collection is predominantly composed of gold jewelry. The complete Thetford hoard comprises twenty-two rings, four bracelets, five chain necklaces, four pendants, two necklace clasps, an amulet, an engraved gem, emerald and glass beads and a belt buckle decorated with a satyr. With the exception of one bracelet, a heavy piece made from two gold rods twisted together, none of the pieces of jewelry appear to have ever been worn. Based on style and design, the jewelry all seems to have come from a single workshop, which may be indicative that this was a merchant's collection, rather than one belonging to an individual who wore any of the items.

Cage cup

300–325 CE
*Glass and copper alloy • Height: 7.4 cm (3 in.),
diameter: 12.2 cm (4¾ in.) • From Germany*

CORNING MUSEUM OF GLASS, NEW YORK, USA

The Roman cage cup, or diatretum, was an expensive,
luxury item that first came to prominence around
250 CE and continued to be popular for the display of
wealth through the 4th century CE. Glass was cut and
ground back to leave only a decorative 'cage' at the
original surface level, usually in a geometric design.
Part of the difficulty of making such an item was that
a small crack or break could destroy the entire piece.
This one, with metal fittings at the base and sides,
suggests it was hung and used as a lamp rather
than as a drinking vessel.

ART AND PERSONAL ADORNMENT

Tigress and cubs mosaic

4th century CE
*Stone • Height: 1.4 m (4½ ft),
width: 1.3 m (4¼ ft) • From
the eastern Empire*

CLEVELAND MUSEUM
OF ART, USA

Scenes depicting animals – particularly large cats suckling or playing with their cubs – were a popular decorative motif in late antiquity, taking over, to some degree, from scenes of hunting. This floor mosaic depicts a mother tiger with three cubs on a white background. Although the mother looks as though she may be growling at the cub in front of her, whose head is turned to face her in a similar gesture, the presence of a cub climbing over her back makes this a playful scene. The tigers are picked out in detail, with polychromatic tesserae of beige, brown, black and yellow used to show patterns and stripes in their fur.

Mirror

4th century CE

Silver • Diameter: 13.2 cm (5¼ in.) • Provenance unknown

METROPOLITAN MUSEUM OF ART, NEW YORK CITY, USA

Produced in the 4th century CE, this mirror follows a design first seen in the 1st century BCE and used continuously throughout antiquity. The style was adopted for use in Asia Minor and the Near East, where it was used until the 9th or 10th century. A mirror such as this had a horizontal handle attached to the rear. This one uses leaves as a decorative motif for attaching the handle, a long-standing Classical feature, and has a Hercules knot at the centre of the handle. The only other decoration is a wreath around the rim, incised into the silver.

Glass goblet

4th century CE
Green glass • Height: 8.5 cm (3¼ in.) • From Ukraine
METROPOLITAN MUSEUM OF ART,
NEW YORK CITY, USA

This blown-glass goblet is made of a pale, translucent green glass; it has a rounded rim and straight sides rounding at the base. It is attached to a globe stem and conical foot, both of which are hollow. It shows some wear from use. Although of 4th-century CE Roman production, the painted decoration of a garland is not ancient and was added at an unknown later date. This may indicate that the goblet was reused by someone unaware of the provenance or antiquity of the glass.

Octagonal pendant featuring Constantine

c. 324–326 CE

*Gold • Pendant height: 9.7 cm (3¾ in.), width: 9.4 cm
(3¾ in.) • From the eastern Empire*

CLEVELAND MUSEUM OF ART, USA

This pendant and two links are all that remains of a larger gold necklace.
The links are fashioned like Corinthian columns. The pendant was
made using a coin of the emperor Constantine as its central feature.
The coin, a rare issue, features the emperor in profile on the obverse,
and his two sons on the reverse. Surrounding the coin are eight
alternating male and female busts in medallions, some of which are
identifiable as mythological figures. This seems slightly incongruous
with Constantine's status as the first Christian emperor, but demonstrates
the melding of two conflicting religious practices in the Roman world
in the 3rd and 4th centuries CE. The necklace was probably owned by
a member of the imperial family or a high-ranking official.

Belt buckle

late 4th–early 5th century CE
*Bronze • Length: 10 cm (4 in.) • From
Catterick Roman Fort, Yorkshire, UK*
BRITISH MUSEUM, LONDON

This stylized bronze buckle was a
typical element of the uniform of
a Roman officer or high-ranking
civil servant in Roman Britain. Sea
horses are flanked by dolphins, a
very popular trope for buckles at this
time. Multiple buckles decorated with
dolphins, probably representative of
the sea gods Oceanus and Neptune,
have been found across Britain and
northern France in connection with
Roman military sites. Excavation of
a cemetery of Roman soldiers near
Leicester in the East Midlands of
England in 2016 produced another
example of a dolphin buckle from the
4th century CE. This particular buckle
combines the two most common
shapes, which were usually either
a square or a loop.

Diptych of Stilicho, Serena and Eucherlus

c. 395 CE
*Ivory • Height: 33 cm (13 in.),
width: 16 cm (6¼ in.), depth: 0.9 cm
(¼ in.) • Provenance unknown*

MONZA CATHEDRAL, ITALY

During the ongoing upheaval in the German provinces in the late 4th and early 5th centuries CE, a Vandal by the name of Stilicho served as general and de facto ruler of the western Roman Empire on behalf of the emperor Honorius. Despite initial success fighting off the Goths, his losses to other barbarian tribes in the Rhine and Danube regions saw him fall from favour. He was executed in 408 CE, and his wife and son were killed soon after. This ivory diptych shows the family in better times; Stilicho is depicted as a tall, well-armed man, indicating his power and authority. His son is shown holding a book, indicating his education, and his Roman wife is depicted holding a flower.

Colossal statue of Constantine

4th century CE

*Marble • Original height of statue: 12.2 m (40 ft),
height of head: 2.6 m (8½ ft) • From Rome, Italy*

CAPITOLINE MUSEUMS, ROME, ITALY

The head, a hand, a foot and portions of an arm and leg
are all that remain of a massive statue of the emperor
Constantine. When complete, the seated statue reached
a height of more than 12 m (40 ft). While the outer limbs
and head were carved from white marble, the torso
consisted of a brick core and wooden frame, gilded in
bronze. The statue was originally located in the Basilica
of Constantine on the edge of the Roman Forum. The
basilica was actually constructed by and initially named
for Maxentius, but after his defeat by Constantine for sole
control of the Empire, the building was rededicated and
statues of Constantine installed in the apse.

SARCOPHAGUS OF HELENA

4th century CE
Porphyry • Height: 1.5 m (5 ft), length: 2.7 m (8¾ ft),
depth: 1.8 m (6 ft) • From Via Labicana, near Rome, Italy
PIO-CLEMENTINO MUSEUM, VATICAN MUSEUMS,
ROME, ITALY

Made of porphyry, an Egyptian red marble that was popular with the imperial family at this time, this sarcophagus contains the remains of Helena, the mother of the emperor Constantine. It is decorated with scenes of a military nature; the sides are carved with Roman soldiers on horseback riding above captured barbarians. On the lid of the sarcophagus there are figures of cupids and victories that hold garlands, while on the very top there are two lions; one sleeping, the other lying down. The decoration is not really suitable for a female burial, leading scholars to conclude the sarcophagus was originally intended for Helena's husband or son and was repurposed when she died unexpectedly in *c.* 328 CE.

The sarcophagus was interred in a mausoleum built by Constantine near the Via Labicana, about 5 km (3 miles) from Rome. The structure was round with a domed roof originally more than 25 m (82 ft) high, punctuated with arcaded windows. The dome was made using broken amphora in order to make it physically lighter. Partially collapsed now, the visible potsherds (pottery shards) gave the tomb its name, Tor Pignattara (Tower of the Vases). This monument, like the sarcophagus itself, was originally meant for Constantine instead of his mother.

By Roman law, burial took place outside the city walls, so that by the imperial period the roads radiating out from Rome were filled with funerary monuments. The Sarcophagus of Helena came from a tomb on the Via Labicana, similar to the Via Appia shown in this etching.

Roman 'Swiss army knife' tool

c. 200–300 CE
*Silver and iron • Height: 8.8 cm (3½ in.), length: 15.5 cm
(6 in.) • Provenance unknown*
FITZWILLIAM MUSEUM, CAMBRIDGE, UK

Incredibly similar to the modern concept of the
Swiss army knife, this iron and silver knife was a
multifunctional tool that would likely have been used
by travellers as well as members of the army. As well
as a knife, a spoon and a fork, this implement provides
a spike, a spatula and a small pick. Folding knives such
as this were not uncommon, but were usually made of
iron or bronze. The incorporation of silver suggests it
was a luxury item used by someone of wealth, such as
a military commander or a merchant.

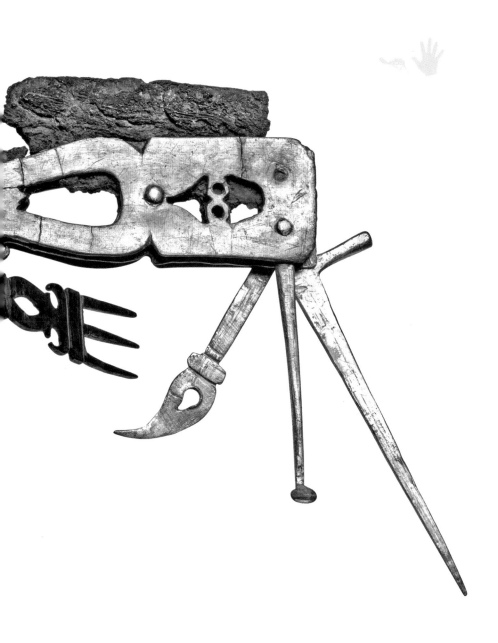

Jonah under the gourd vine

late 3rd century CE
Marble • Height: 32.3 cm (12¾ in.), length: 46.3 cm (18¼ in.), depth: 18 cm (7 in.) • From Asia Minor

CLEVELAND MUSEUM OF ART, USA

This statue illustrates an episode in the Book of Jonah in the Old Testament of the Bible. In the story, Jonah awaits the destruction of the city of Nineveh by God as punishment for the wicked behaviour of the inhabitants. Distrusting their attempts to change, he waits some distance from the city, watching. God causes a vine to grow to protect Jonah from the sun and wind of the desert, but then it wilts as Jonah continues to call God's judgment into question. As the Book of Jonah is from the Old Testament (Torah), the statue could be Jewish or Christian, but the style and material suggest a Romanized origin, which makes it more likely to be Christian.

BOWL BASE WITH CHRIST GIVING MARTYRS' CROWNS TO SAINT PETER AND SAINT PAUL

c. 350 CE

Glass and gold leaf • Height: 13.8 cm (5½ in.), width: 12.5 cm (5 in.), depth: 5 cm (2 in.) • From Rome, Italy

METROPOLITAN MUSEUM OF ART, NEW YORK CITY, USA

Only a fragment of the base of this bowl remains, embedded in the mortar in which it was found when excavated. The figures of Peter and Paul are identified by name, and the Latin text running around the edge of the base says 'joyful in Christ, worthy among thy friends'. Christ, the central figure, is shown giving a crown to both Peter and Paul. This is identified as one of five crowns mentioned in the Bible, the crown of life, also known as the martyr's crown. This crown was awarded to those who endured severe hardship, testing, tribulation and/or physical death on behalf of God.

The technique by which this bowl was made, called gold sandwich glass, was incredibly popular in the 3rd and 4th centuries CE. Made by fusing gold leaf between two pieces of glass, the gold glass was bright and reflective, and gave a lustrous quality to whatever it was used for. Small pieces of gold glass (largely appropriated from bigger objects) were used to decorate individual burials in the catacombs of Rome. The use of gold glass in early Christian art created an association between it and depictions of religious themes that continued through the Byzantine period and into the Middle Ages.

Gold sandwich glass was used to make tesserae for mosaics, creating the brilliant gold mosaics typical of the Christian/ Byzantine period, and used throughout the Middle Ages. This mosaic depicting Christ, from the Hagia Sophia, Istanbul, Turkey, is an example of the bright, glowing appearance made possible by the gold tesserae.

Bowl with Saints Peter and Paul

c. 350 CE

Terracotta • Height: 8.5 cm (3¼ in.), diameter: 14 cm (5½ in.) • From Rome, Italy

METROPOLITAN MUSEUM OF ART, NEW YORK CITY, USA

Found in a catacomb on the Via Appia in Rome, this fairly simple ceramic bowl imitates the more expensive saintly items produced in gold glass. The saints Peter and Paul, who are identified by name in Latin, are shown facing each other, with the chi-rho between their heads. The exterior of the bowl is decorated with a band of Christograms framed with martyrs' wreaths. This bowl, simple though it is, combines a number of Paleochristian elements in a single item. This illustrates how quickly the iconography of Christianity spread across the Empire and among all socio-economic levels.

Chi-rho dish

c. 370 CE

Pewter • Dimensions: unknown • From Venta Silurum (modern Caerwent), Wales, UK

NEWPORT MUSEUM AND ART GALLERY, WALES, UK

Venta Silurum (present-day Caerwent in south-east Wales) was a Roman administrative centre founded around 75 CE. This pewter dish was found along with a number of other kitchen items in the ruins of a house near the town's forum. Inscribed on the base of the dish is the chi-rho, a symbol used by early Christians consisting of the first two letters of Christ's name in Greek superimposed over each other to make a single form. This dish is among the earliest artefacts of Christianity in the British Isles, where evidence of the new religion begins to appear around 370 CE.

Spoon with Saint Paul as an athlete

c. 350–400 CE
Silver • Height: 5.6 cm (2¼ in.),
width: 4.6 cm (1¾ in.) • From Syria
CLEVELAND MUSEUM
OF ART, USA

This silver spoon seems to
have a somewhat unusual
subject, depicting Saint Paul
as an athlete. The figure,
nude and with well-defined
musculature, wears a crown
and holds a stalk, a pose typical
of an athlete victorious at
Roman games. He is identified
by name, however, giving this
object a decidedly Christian slant.
It may be a reference to one of
Paul's letters to the Corinthians,
in which he identifies himself as an
athlete of Christ. A personal object
made for use or display in the home,
it must have been the possession of
a Christian. The swan neck handles
were popular on spoons in the late
imperial period.

Signet ring with Christian motif

5th century CE
*Gold • Diameter: 2.6 cm
(1 in.), weight: 28.8 g (1 oz)
• Provenance unknown*

BRITISH MUSEUM,
LONDON, UK

This gold signet ring is composed of a square bezel and a ring constructed of seven small medallions, between each of which are two small granules. The bezel is decorated with a man and a woman, both dressed as wealthy Romans of the late antique period. Between them is an equal-armed cross, which provides the religious context for the jewelry. The medallions that form the ring are engraved with alternating male and female heads surrounded by floral garlands. The men wear a stylized crossbow fibula and the women are shown with necklaces and earrings. It is likely one of a pair of marriage rings. Due to its large size, it is probably the male ring.

Glossary

Antefix a vertical block that terminates the covering tiles of the roof. It conceals the foot of the row of convex tiles that covers the joints of the flat tiles. In grand buildings, it is typically decorated.

Anthropomorphic ascribing human form or attributes to a being or thing not human, especially in relation to a deity or animal.

Apse a semicircular or polygonal termination or recess in a building, usually vaulted with a domed roof. A typical feature in both Roman public and private buildings, it is now more commonly seen in churches.

Askos (pl. askoi) a squat jar for wine or oil. It resembles a wineskin in shape, with an ellipsoidal body and a short spout at one or both ends that could also be used as a handle. Typically, it was used for pouring small amounts of liquid as a libation.

Bezel a groove that holds the stone of a gem in its setting.

Biconical an object that consists of two cones placed with their bases meeting to form a single structure.

Brazier a portable heater. It comprises a pan or stand for holding lighted coals or wood and could be used either for heating or for cooking food. Found in a funerary context, it was most likely employed to cook a funeral meal.

Bucchero a distinctly black burnished ceramic ware, distinguished by its glossy surface. It is identified as an indigenous Etruscan material that is associated exclusively with the pre-Roman culture of northern Italy.

Cartouche a carved tablet, drawing or frame that represents a scroll with rolled-up ends, used ornamentally or bearing an inscription.

Cista a box or basket utilized by the ancient Egyptians, Greeks, Etruscans and Romans for various practical and mystical purposes.

Consul two annually elected chief magistrates who jointly ruled the Republic.

Damnatio Memoriae the public condemnation and erasure of a person's name and image after their death, thus removing their memory from public life.

Filigree ornamental metalwork of fine wire, formed into delicate tracery.

Granulation manufacturing technique in which metal is formed into small grains or spheres before being added to the base, usually of the same metal.

Impasto the process or technique of laying on paint or pigment thickly so that it stands out from a surface.

Intaglio a design incised or engraved into a material, usually gemstones.

Kantharos a deep bowl on a stem. Two handles rise

from the brim and curve downwards to join the body. Used for drinking.

Kore (pl. korai) an ancient Greek statue of a young woman standing and clothed in long loose robes.

Lararium a small shrine in the home for the worshipping of the household gods.

Lebes (pl. lebetes) a type of ancient Greek cauldron, normally in bronze.

Libation a pouring out of wine or other liquid in honour of a deity or deceased relative.

Nenfro a type of volcanic rock found in the Viterbo region of northern Lazio, used by the Etruscans for making sculptures.

Nymphaeum a room containing a fountain, adorned with plants and sculptures. It served as a place of rest, a grotto or a shrine dedicated to a nymph or nymphs.

Orientalizing style influenced by the Near East and Asia Minor. The style included the use of animal and floral themes, particularly marked by the inclusion of sphinxes, lions and lotuses.

Palmettes an ornament of radiating petals that resembles a palm leaf.

Punic Wars a series of three wars fought between Rome and Carthage between 264 and 146 BCE.

Pyxis a small box or casket, usually cylindrical in shape. It has a lid with a central knob.

Repoussé decorative technique in which metal is ornamented or shaped by hammering from the reverse side to create a design in low relief.

Scarab a stone or faience beetle used in ancient Egypt as a talisman, ornament and symbol of resurrection.

Semitic a family of languages that includes Hebrew, Arabic and Aramaic as well as certain ancient languages such as Phoenician and Akkadian.

Stela (pl. stelae) an upright stone slab or column. Typically, it bears a commemorative inscription or decorative relief, and often serves as a gravestone.

Symposium a convivial meeting for drinking and intellectual conversation, usually held after a dinner.

Terra sigillata also known as Samian ware. It is a fine red pottery with a glossy surface and stamped decoration. Produced in specific areas of the western Roman Empire.

Triclinium a dining room, so-called because it typically contained three moveable couches (clinia) on which diners would recline during the meal.

Trompe l'oeil a visual illusion in art, used to trick the eye into perceiving a painted detail as a three-dimensional object.

Tumulus (pl. tumuli) an ancient burial mound usually comprised of stones topped with earth.

Venetic an extinct Indo-European language that was spoken in northeast Italy and part of modern Slovenia in antiquity.

Volutes a spiral scroll that features in Ionic, Corinthian and composite capitals of columns.

Votive an object offered or consecrated in fulfilment of a vow.

Zoomorphic Representing or imitating the form of an animal.

Index

*Page numbers in **bold** refer to illustrations*

Museum Index

AUSTRIA
Vienna
Kunsthistorisches Museum
chain with fifty-two pendants 242–243

DENMARK
Copenhagen
National Museum of Denmark
circus cup 161
Ny Carlsberg Glyptotek
portrait of Vespasian 186

FRANCE
Lyons
Lyons Museum of Fine Arts
coin of Vercingetorix 116
Paris
Louvre
bust of Livia 180–181
engraved hand mirror 90
Etruscan pendant with swastika symbols 28
Portrait of a woman 212–213
Praetorians Relief 182–183
National Library of France
Great Cameo of France, The 164–165

GERMANY
Bad Homburg
Saalburg Museum
planes for woodworking 193
Berlin
Antikensammlung, Berlin State Museums
Severan Tondo 192
Koblenz
Koblenz State Museum
Dacian Draco standard 202–203

Munich
Munich Glyptothek
bust of Lucius Cornelius Sulla 121
Trier
Rhineland Archaeologial Museum
Neumagen wine ship tombstone 209
relief depicting making bread 226–227

GREECE
Athens
Museum of the Ancient Agora
rules of the Library of Pantainos 152
Delphi
Delphi Archaeological Museum
statue of Antinous 189

ISRAEL
Jerusalem
Israel Museum
house keys from Cave of Letters 156

ITALY
Bologna
Archaeological Civic Museum of Bologna
askos 49
candelabrum with Aeneas and
    Anchises 75
carved throne 40–41
funeral stela 48
Zannoni stela 54
Ercolano
Herculaneum Archaeological Park
Neptune and Amphitrite mosaic 140
Este
National Museum of Atestino
votive tablet with Venetic alphabet 50–51
Ferrara
National Archaeological Museum of Ferrara
zoomorphic rhyta 126–127
Florence
National Archaeological Museum of Florence
Chimera of Arezzo, The 85
votive uterus 129

Picture Credits

All works are courtesy of the museums listed in the individual captions.

Acknowledgments

My utmost gratitude to Joanne Berry for thinking of me for this project, and to Katherine McDonald, Matthew Nicholls, and Jonathan Prag for assisting me with elements of their own research. I also wish to thank Hannah Phillips for her patience and support throughout the writing process. Finally, in this and all things, I am indebted to my parents for all that they do, and to Nathan Morris, whose faith in me is unwavering.

First published in the United Kingdom in 2017 by
Thames & Hudson Ltd, 181A High Holborn,
London WC1V 7QX

© 2017 Quintessence Editions Ltd.

This book was designed and produced by
Quintessence Editions Ltd.
The Old Brewery
6 Blundell Street
London N7 9BH

Project Editor	Hannah Phillips
Senior Designer	Isabel Eeles
Researcher	Helen Murphy-Smith
Picture Researcher	Kate Duncan
Production Manager	Anna Pauletti
Editorial Director	Ruth Patrick
Publisher	Philip Cooper

British Library Cataloguing-in-Publication Data
A catalogue record for this book is available from the British Library

ISBN 978-0-500-51959-2

Printed and bound in China